MIRIAM STOPPARD

MY
FIRST FOOD
BOOK

DORLING KINDERSLEY · LONDON

For
Lorena Romelia, Memuna and Radha

Editor
Carolyn Ryden
Consultant Editor
Charyn Jones
Designer
Joanna Martin

Managing Editor
Daphne Razazan
Art Director
Anne-Marie Bulat

Photography
Martin Brigdale

First published in Great Britain in 1987 by
Dorling Kindersley Publishers Limited,
9 Henrietta Street, London WC2E 8PS
Second impression 1987
Third impression 1988
Copyright © 1986 by
Dorling Kindersley Limited, London
Text copyright © 1986 by Miriam Stoppard

British Library Cataloguing in Publication Data
Stoppard, Miriam
My First Food Book
I Cookery   II Infants – Nutrition
I Title
641.5'622   TX652
ISBN 0-86318-170-8

Printed in Hong Kong

ONTENTS

INTRODUCTION *Page 4*

EVERYDAY MEALS
TELL-THE-TIME-BREAKFAST *Page 6*
CEREALS *Page 7*
SUNSHINE BREAKFAST *Page 8*
BREADS *Page 9*

EGG SAIL-BOATS *Page 10*
CAT AND MOUSE *Page 11*
SMILEY FACE PIZZA *Page 12*
CHEESY MONSTER *Page 13*
FISH FINGER TREE *Page 14*
FUNNY FISH *Page 15*
TUNA POTATO BOAT *Page 16*

JUMPING PRAWNS *Page 17*
CHICKEN CHEWS *Page 18*
TASTY TEDDY BEAR *Page 19*
MERRY MEATBALL PONY *Page 20*
RATTLE MUNCH *Page 21*
MEAT LOAF MOTOR CAR *Page 22*
SOUPS *Page 23*
LIVER LOG CABIN *Page 24*
LITTLE SURPRISES *Page 25*
PICK-UP PASTA BOAT *Page 26*
TRAFFIC LIGHTS *Page 27*
POLKA-DOT OCTOPUS *Page 28*
BEANY RING *Page 29*
BIRD'S NEST FEAST *Page 30*

DRINKS *Page 31*
LEAFY PARCEL TRAIN *Page 32*
VEGETABLE ROCKET *Page 33*
STICKMAN FEAST *Page 34*
DIP IDEAS *Page 35*
STIR-FRIED KITE *Page 36*
SANDWICH MAN *Page 37*
PASTIE CRAB *Page 38*
SAVOURY CONE *Page 39*
QUICHE FLOWER *Page 40*
BAKING *Page 41*
FOODS FOR TEETHERS *Page 42*
FOOD ON THE MOVE *Page 44*
PICNIC FOOD *Page 45*

SPECIAL OCCASIONS
EASTER FEAST *Page 46*
EASTER TREATS *Page 47*
CHRISTMAS DINNER *Page 48*
CHRISTMAS TREATS *Page 49*
BIRTHDAY PARTY *Page 50*
SWEETS AND TREATS *Page 51*

FOOD FACTS
FACTS ON FRUIT AND VEGETABLES
Page 52
WHAT TO INTRODUCE WHEN *Page 54*
RECIPES *Page 56*
INDEX AND ACKNOWLEDGMENTS
Page 64

INTRODUCTION

When it comes to feeding young children, one of the mistakes parents often make is to impose adult appetites and eating habits on to them. For instance, most of us believe that children, like adults, need to eat three square meals a day. This is not so. Some children are perfectly healthy and happy on two meals or even one bumper meal a day with lots of healthy snacks in between. Just as many children eat sparingly as eat heartily and even this set pattern can change if your child is going through a growth spurt or is feeling off-colour. Babies, like animals, are self-regulating, so try to be flexible and let them take the lead, up to a point!

Why first foods are important

There is no question that a child's diet is important because first foods and tastes form the building blocks for his or her future diet and health. But don't let food become an obsession. If you're too anxious about what and how much your child eats, mealtimes will become miserable battlegrounds.

Here are some basic rules to follow when you are trying to tempt young eaters. Pay attention to texture: when children are teething their gums are sensitive and they are learning to use their mouths, their teeth and their tongues. Crunchy foods served with soft puréed foods provide good variety at this time. Use fruit and vegetables to make meals look colourful as well as for the different nutrients these provide. Steam or stir-fry vegetables as much as you can so they retain their colour and flavour and serve some of them raw as chewy instant snacks. Remember to keep portions small so your child does not feel put off by the quantity. Better to give seconds than have a pile of rejected food. Always let foods cool right down before serving as young children's mouths are particularly sensitive to temperature and can be easily burned.

Eating patterns

Children's appetites are notoriously fickle: they're easily distracted from their food and they may have a fad for certain foods for days or even weeks on end. We so often make the mistake of thinking in terms of a 24-hour cycle and this just doesn't exist for babies and small children. So don't get upset when your child rejects a meal; he will probably eat heartily at the next. Even if he rejects certain foods for weeks at a time, he is likely to get the essential nutrients from elsewhere, as long as you serve a wide variety of foods.

From the time they can feed themselves, the majority of children want fairly frequent meals or snacks consisting of small amounts of food with different textures and colours. In this book we show simply cooked, nutritious meals arranged in recognizable, picture-book shapes and patterns – often helped by the use of cookie cutters and moulds – to encourage your child to eat well. You'll find that you can make foods look appealing with very little effort. Don't spend too much of your time creating elaborate arrangements or you'll feel even more depressed and resentful when pieces are thrown on the floor. Instead, treat these shapes as a catalogue of ideas to encourage your child to enjoy eating, to try new foods and to have fun at mealtimes.

Mealtimes

It is important to bring an open mind to feeding children so that you don't put undue pressure on them and make mealtimes unhappy. Mealtimes should be relaxed and sociable occasions. After the initial weaning process, your child should eat the family's food with the family as often as possible to establish a pleasant routine and to get an early training in good table behaviour. But do keep rules and restrictions at mealtimes to a minimum.

Help yourself by using a plastic bib and putting newspaper or plastic on the floor underneath the high chair so that you can scoop up any jettisoned food at the end of the meal. The sooner you let children feed themselves with fingers or a spoon, the sooner they become adept at getting the food into their mouths without too much mess. This is part of the attraction of finger foods; not only do they encourage independence and learning, they also give you time to enjoy your meal. But don't expect your child to be able to feed himself an entire meal. Some food is bound to end up on the floor and in the bib. You will have to help some of the time at first. However, if you try to allow your child some independence, mealtimes will be more fun for you too. But don't be tempted to leave your child alone when he is eating: it is so quick and easy for a young child to choke and you should always be on hand in case something goes down the wrong way.

Healthier eating habits

You may have to make some changes in your cooking habits when preparing food for a young child. For example, no salt should be added during or after cooking because of the strain it puts on young kidneys and also to encourage a taste for real food and not a taste for salt. Try to be aware of precisely what you are feeding your child. This applies whenever you serve anything but fresh, raw foods. All the foods in this book are wholesome and free from artificial additives. This is now easier to monitor with the labelling system on commercial products. Read labels carefully. They often include scientific-sounding 'E' numbers but these are not necessarily chemicals, some are natural ingredients and

quite safe, so do try to find out what the 'E' numbers stand for. When reading labels, take a note of the order of the ingredients too. They are listed in descending order of proportion with the main constituent first. If water is top of the list, water is the main ingredient.

We should all cut down on our salt intake and the amount of sugar and saturated fats we consume, so perhaps this is a time in your life when you too can try to eat a more healthy, wholefood-based diet, if you don't already do so. We recommend some foods that you may only have seen in healthfood shops. Tofu, for example, can be an ideal food for babies and young children because it supplies a wide range of nutrients quickly and easily. It is tasteless and smooth in texture but when cooked it absorbs other flavours well. Try it and experiment, you might be pleasantly surprised.

How the book is planned

We have set out to inspire you with some wonderful shapes and ideas based on finger foods for children aged from 9 months. Each meal is nutritionally balanced and in most cases can be adapted from the foods you use and prepare for the rest of the family. We haven't featured a drink with every meal. You can provide a diluted fruit juice or, better still, water, if your child is thirsty. Recipes for most of the dishes are given at the back of the book, where there is also a food introduction chart to give you some idea of what you can be feeding your child and when. There are also general guidelines and hints on using fruit and vegetables, storing food and how to avoid allergic reactions. I hope that the combination of fun shapes, nutritious ingredients and different flavours will make these meals winners every time, both for you and for your child.

TELL-THE-TIME BREAKFAST

Egg, bread, soft cheese and fruit combine in a clock shape to form this breakfast. Older children will enjoy eating their way round the clock as they try to tell the time. Younger ones will simply like the shape. The bread pieces are dipped in beaten egg with a spoonful of milk. After immersing the bread to get it thoroughly coated, fry it quickly in a non-stick frying pan brushed with a little oil. For a quicker meal, simply spread pieces of bread with peanut butter, jam or soft cheese and chopped fruit. Fruit is a good instant food, even at breakfast time, and you should try to serve a few slices of fresh fruit every day, as snacks and with meals.

Slices of watermelon, peeled and seeded

Ricotta cheese and chopped dried apricot

Breakfast clock face
Twelve pieces of bread, some topped with a cheese spread, others dipped in egg and lightly fried, arranged as a clock.

Banana clock hands

CEREALS

White rice has bran removed but is good in milk puddings.

Brown rice is high in vitamins, minerals and fibre.

Pot barley is good in soups and has a pleasant chewy texture.

Commercial baby rice is the best starter cereal and least allergenic.

We should all eat more whole grain cereals and by including them in your child's diet from very early on, you may come to eat more yourself. For most babies, their first solid food is an iron-rich commercial baby cereal. However, you can make your own mixes and grind them in a blender to get a finer texture. Use rice, oats, barley, rye, millet and wheat. Add dried or fresh fruit and ground nuts, and serve combined with milk, yogurt or diluted apple juice. When you buy ready-to-eat brands, always read the labels carefully. Few are free of salt and sugar but if you shop around you should find some suitable brands. Don't limit cereals to breakfast time, use them in all your cooking, as a topping, a thickener, a coating and when you bake.

Bulgar wheat requires soaking but little cooking and tastes nutty.

Commercial breakfast cereal. Check labels to avoid added sugar.

Millet cooks to a mush and is high in valuable nutrients.

Ground muesli. Grind your own mix and soak or cook in liquid to soften before serving.

Cornmeal makes bright yellow bread and a crunchy coating.

Semolina is made from wheat and is good in puddings.

Rolled oats are good as porridge and in biscuits.

SUNSHINE BREAKFAST

Every household has a different idea of what the traditional breakfast should be, but with young children, who are usually ravenous when they wake up in the mornings, speed has to be the main consideration. This breakfast makes a change from the usual cereal and it needn't take long to prepare. Drop scones can be made in batches and then frozen. To serve, simply toast them lightly so they heat through. The addition of dried fruit provides extra vitamins, fibre and iron. Slices of fresh orange, carefully peeled, are juicy and full of vitamin C. You may want to cut them in half for younger children to eat.

Orange segments
When serving oranges to very young children, remove all peel, pith and pips so there is no risk of choking.

Drop scone
A drop scone cooked with raisins and dried apricot. Alternatively, top with slices of fresh fruit or cheese. *Recipe: p.60.*

Raisins

Dried apricot

Plain oat biscuit
Good for fibre and texture. Spread with soft cheese or fruit purée for variety and extra flavour. *Recipe: p.62.*

BREADS

Pumpernickel rye bread

Granary bread.
The grains
may be too
tough for
young babies

French bread

Irish soda
bread

Wholemeal bread is the best to serve your child but there are many other high fibre, wholegrain breads available. If your child eats these most of the time, the occasional slice of white bread is fine. You can make any bread look more attractive by cutting it into shapes using cookie cutters and serving it with different spreads. Always read the label carefully when buying packaged bread. Some brown breads are not wholemeal at all and contain colouring agents. If you bake your own bread, try to use 100% wholemeal flour and experiment with wheatgerm, sesame seeds and bran for extra flavour.

Polish rye bread
with caraway seeds

Cornbread
(Recipe: p.60.)

Wholemeal bread spread
with strawberry jam

Fruit bread

Black rye bread

EGG SAIL-BOATS

Although eggs are a good source of protein and iron you should introduce them gradually: first the yolk, then the white when your child is 10–12 months old. Check for any possible reaction (see p.55), and use sparingly in your child's diet. Three or four eggs a week is about right for young children so if you use eggs a lot in cooking, provide slices rather than halves when serving these sail-boats. Add a portion of wholemeal bread and a tempting vegetable. Mangetout, here stuffed with cottage cheese, are tender and fun to eat. Alternatively, fill lettuce hearts, or lightly steamed or raw celery sticks with the fibrous strands removed.

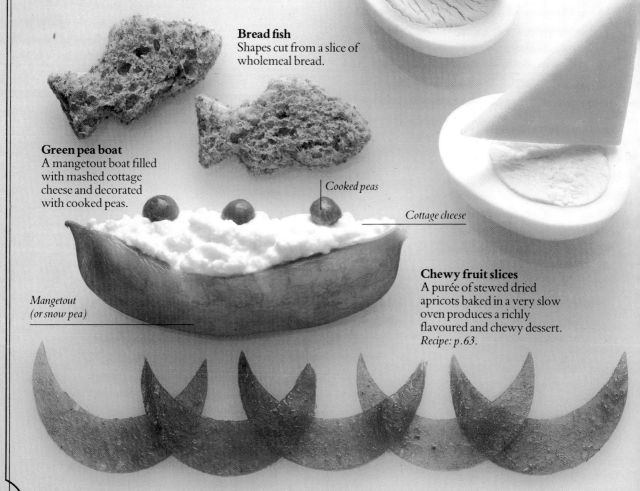

Hard-boiled egg

Gouda cheese

Egg sail-boats
A hard-boiled egg, halved, with triangles of Gouda cheese. Make an incision in the egg to secure the cheese sails.

Bread fish
Shapes cut from a slice of wholemeal bread.

Green pea boat
A mangetout boat filled with mashed cottage cheese and decorated with cooked peas.

Cooked peas

Cottage cheese

Mangetout (or snow pea)

Chewy fruit slices
A purée of stewed dried apricots baked in a very slow oven produces a richly flavoured and chewy dessert.
Recipe: p.63.

CAT AND MOUSE

If your child has been introduced to a cat, or a story about a cat and a mouse, these shapes will be particularly interesting. A simple one-egg omelette has slices of boiled potato and fresh parsley added to it. Parsley is rich in calcium, iron and vitamins. Serve it finely chopped as a garnish to add colour to any meal. Use whatever vegetables you have available to fill the omelette so that it holds its shape. Add extra flavour and texture with herbs, cheese or crunchy beansprouts. Cut the omelette into strips and then push back into shape before decorating and serving so your child can pick up and eat the pieces as a finger food.

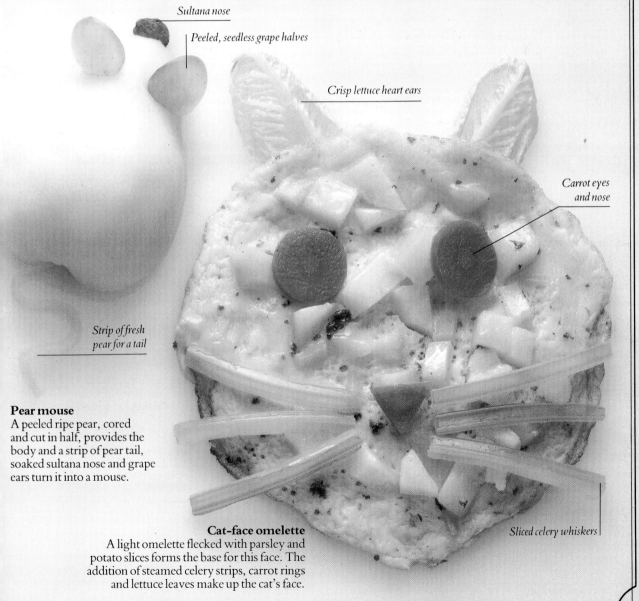

Sultana nose

Peeled, seedless grape halves

Crisp lettuce heart ears

Carrot eyes and nose

Strip of fresh pear for a tail

Pear mouse
A peeled ripe pear, cored and cut in half, provides the body and a strip of pear tail, soaked sultana nose and grape ears turn it into a mouse.

Cat-face omelette
A light omelette flecked with parsley and potato slices forms the base for this face. The addition of steamed celery strips, carrot rings and lettuce leaves make up the cat's face.

Sliced celery whiskers

SMILEY FACE PIZZA

Pizza is a favourite meal for all the family and can be prepared in individual portions for your child. You can make it with a traditional yeast dough or a simple scone dough as here. For extra speed, use a halved muffin or a slice of pitta bread as a base. Gently toast one side, put some grated cheese on the other, spread on the topping, decorate and grill. The basic pizza topping of tomatoes, minced onions and cheese can be livened up for the rest of the family with tuna fish, anchovies, or olives. Keep your child's portion lighter in flavour and allow it to cool well before serving; cheese retains its heat and can scald a young mouth.

Cress arranged as hair

Mozzarella cheese eyes

Mushroom nose

Pepper slice mouth

Smiley face pizza
An all-in-one meal consisting of a simple pizza decorated with cheese and vegetables and pieces of fresh fruit.
Recipe: p.58.

Water
Water is one of the best drinks to serve at mealtimes. Start early as children soon learn to prefer juices and flavoured drinks.

Peeled kiwi fruit

Peeled, seedless grape

CHEESY MONSTER

This friendly monster is made from a simple, tasty cheese and lentil bake, cut into shapes and decorated. Lentils are economical, quick to cook and highly nutritious. They mix well with any cooked vegetable and make a protein-rich meal when served in combination with cheese, egg and wholemeal breadcrumbs. A blend of Quark and raspberry purée provides a dip-style dessert that can be sucked off biscuits, fruit slices or even fingers.

Cheesy monster
Arranged from cheese and lentil bake with slices of steamed courgette for limbs.
Recipe: p.59.

Sliced green olive

Tomato purée

Peeled raw apple

Steamed soft courgette for limbs, spine and tail

Raspberry dip
Quark, a low fat cheese made from skimmed milk, mixed with raspberry purée and served with fruit.

CHEESE

Cheese in any form is an excellent food for children, but don't rely solely on traditional hard, high-fat cheeses like Cheddar. Try the medium-fat cheeses such as Edam, Gouda and some of the Swiss and Scandinavian varieties. These are mild in flavour and many have holes, which are interesting to children.

Don't hesitate to introduce the soft French cheeses; Camembert and Brie are often favourites because of their texture and mild flavour. Remove the rind before serving. Soft low-fat cheeses such as cottage cheese, Quark, Ricotta and curd cheese are easy to digest and can be added to dishes in place of milk.

Cheese on toast, penguin shaped

Jarlsberg

Low-fat soft cheese.

Ricotta and chopped apricot

Edam

Grilled Camembert

FISH FINGER TREE

White fish is an excellent source of protein, delicate in flavour, low in fat, soft and easily digested by young children. Try to buy fresh fish and remove the skin and any bones (easier done after cooking). This fish finger is home-made but you can buy some good commercial brands. Check the ingredients on the label and remove any coating if there is artificial colour-ing added. You can make your own attractive coatings with any combination of grains, cereals, seeds and breadcrumbs. Remember to let the grilled fish cool down before serving it.

Steamed broccoli florets

Cherry tomatoes

Fruity flower
A colourful and juicy flower made from slices of ripe honeydew melon and orange segments takes hardly any time to prepare.

Orange slices

Fish finger

Melon ball centre

Fish finger tree
Steamed broccoli and tiny cherry tomatoes arranged around a homemade fish finger to form a tree.
Recipe: p.57.

Edam cheese

Italian breadstick

Melon stem

FUNNY FISH

White fish is such a nutritious food that we should all try to eat more on a regular basis and in a variety of ways. Steam it, bake it with herbs and vegetables, poach it in milk or coat it with a cereal mixture for grilling or baking. Double check that there are no bones present before serving fish. For extra fun, arrange the fish pieces into a shape that your child will recognize. Serve it with crisp and colourful vegetables and chewy foods like these little dried fruit balls. A slice of wholemeal bread is also a good accompaniment. Make it a rule never to leave your child alone when he or she is eating because there is always the risk of choking. Besides, meals should be sociable times and not solitary occasions.

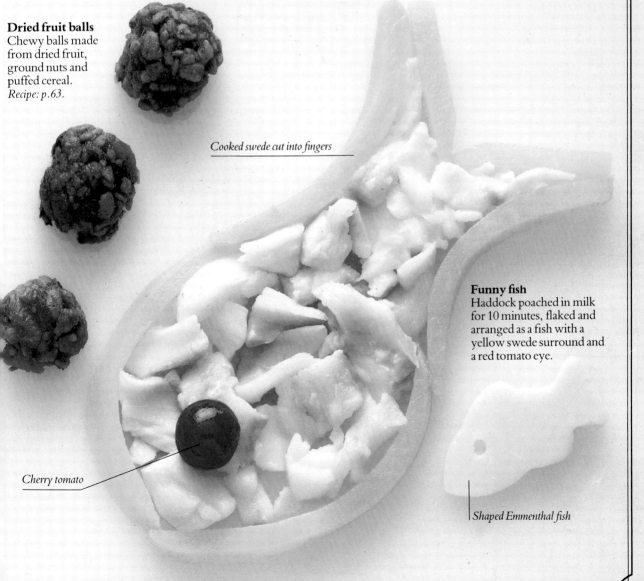

Dried fruit balls
Chewy balls made from dried fruit, ground nuts and puffed cereal.
Recipe: p.63.

Cooked swede cut into fingers

Funny fish
Haddock poached in milk for 10 minutes, flaked and arranged as a fish with a yellow swede surround and a red tomato eye.

Cherry tomato

Shaped Emmenthal fish

TUNA POTATO BOAT

Potatoes, baked in their skins and stuffed with a variety of fillings, served with a few vegetables or a small salad, provide a complete meal. This potato boat is filled with a mixture of potato, tuna and yogurt (cottage or curd cheese or Quark would do just as well). Alternatively, make up a mixture from different sliced vegetables, grated cheese, minced meat or flaked white fish. By the time you have prepared the filling the potato will have cooled down to the right temperature for your child. Dessert consists of fresh fruit slices. Try to serve some fresh fruit with every meal so that it becomes a healthy habit.

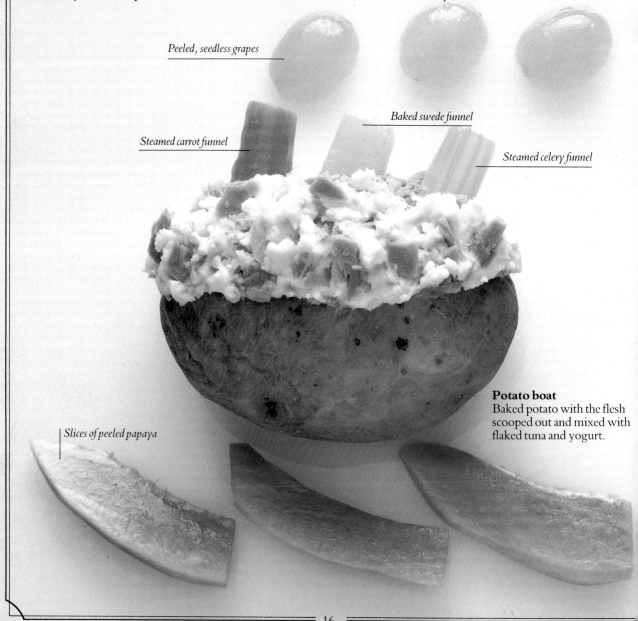

Peeled, seedless grapes

Baked swede funnel

Steamed carrot funnel

Steamed celery funnel

Slices of peeled papaya

Potato boat
Baked potato with the flesh scooped out and mixed with flaked tuna and yogurt.

JUMPING PRAWNS

Prawns are frequently great favourites with children; they're easy to hold, an appealing colour and good to chew. However, you are recommended to avoid serving shellfish to children under 12 months of age as, in some cases, it can cause an allergic reaction if given too early. Tomatoes, like potatoes, make excellent containers. Fill them with any ingredients and serve as a lucky dip. As tomatoes are a rich source of vitamin C and are available all year round, you should try to serve them often in a variety of ways. The fruit pastie is sliced open to make a butterfly shape and show off its colourful filling.

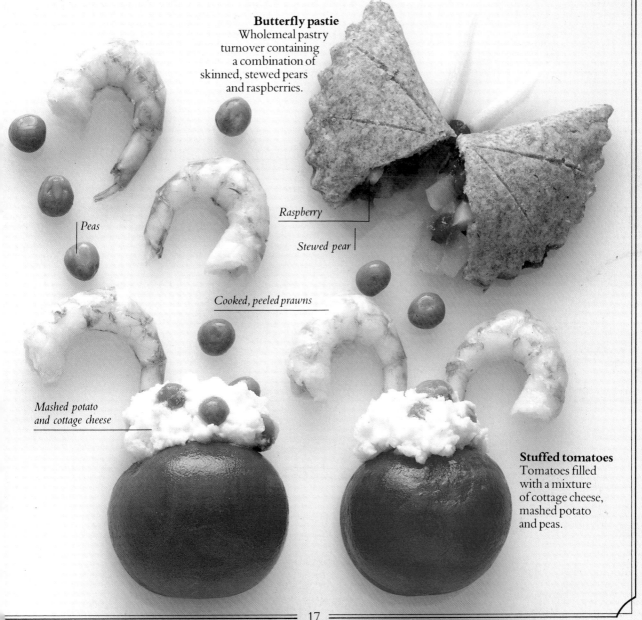

Butterfly pastie
Wholemeal pastry turnover containing a combination of skinned, stewed pears and raspberries.

Raspberry

Stewed pear

Peas

Cooked, peeled prawns

Mashed potato and cottage cheese

Stuffed tomatoes
Tomatoes filled with a mixture of cottage cheese, mashed potato and peas.

CHICKEN CHEWS

Chicken is often the first meat a child samples and it frequently remains a firm favourite. Served in this way it becomes a meal that the whole family will enjoy. Simply cut your child's portion into bite-sized, easy-to-handle pieces and arrange it in a funny shape. Use skinned and boned chicken breasts; it is always important to remove the skin as it can be hard to chew and most of the fat lies immediately beneath it. Coat the meat in beaten egg and a ground cereal mixture or breadcrumbs before baking it. Assorted chopped fruit served in half an orange with the flesh scooped out makes a tempting and colourful fruit salad.

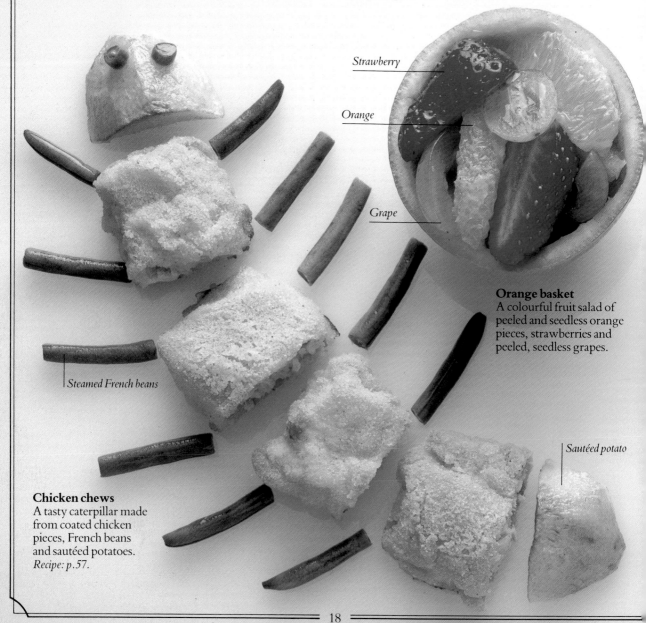

Strawberry

Orange

Grape

Steamed French beans

Sautéed potato

Orange basket
A colourful fruit salad of peeled and seedless orange pieces, strawberries and peeled, seedless grapes.

Chicken chews
A tasty caterpillar made from coated chicken pieces, French beans and sautéed potatoes.
Recipe: p.57.

TASTY TEDDY BEAR

The teddy bear is a favourite shape with all children and one they will recognize from an early age. This is an ideal meal to prepare whenever the family has had chicken or turkey and there are some pieces left over, but don't be tempted to use cooked meat that is more than 24 hours old; it may harbour bacteria. Here, the teddy bear is made from a chopped turkey and mashed potato mixture which is coated in oatmeal and baked in the oven. You can easily adapt the recipe by using a wide variety of ingredients such as flaked fish, mashed cooked pulses or minced lean meat. Serve with any steamed fresh vegetables and juicy fruit slices.

Grapefruit with pith and seeds removed

Slice of peeled mango

Carrot steamed until soft for limbs, face and buttons

Teddy croquette
A favourite toy becomes edible with steamed carrot limbs and turkey croquettes as its body and head.
Recipe: p.57.

MERRY MEATBALL PONY

Small meatballs are an ideal finger food and simple to prepare, particularly if you are making them for the rest of the family. Use best quality minced lean beef or lamb; it is worth it for the flavour and lack of fat. You can bind the meatballs with egg and any number of ingredients such as wheatgerm, wholemeal breadcrumbs or rolled oats and flavour them with grated cheese or herbs. Grill or bake the meatballs to give them a crunchy coating. Steam or stir-fry the accompanying vegetables so that they retain their crispness and colour. To add interest in the dessert, top a cereal biscuit with soft fruit and Ricotta or yogurt.

Stir-fried carrot for ears

Oat biscuit dessert
A homemade biscuit becomes a wholesome dessert when topped with slices of peeled ripe plum and natural yogurt.
Recipe: p. 62.

Natural yogurt

Oat biscuit

Peeled ripe plum

Meatball pony
Three mini meatballs arranged with slices of stir-fried carrot.
Recipe: p. 57.

Stir-fried carrot for legs

Cress for grass

RATTLE MUNCH

To make this extra nutritious beefburger, simply adapt the basic meatball recipe by reshaping the mixture into larger and flatter rounds. Give the beefburger added texture and fibre with a coating of cooked brown rice, barley, rolled oats, wheatgerm or sesame seeds before baking or grilling it. Try to copy the shape of your baby's favourite rattle or toy to make the meal doubly tempting. As most children enjoy meat presented in this way, serve it with vegetables that are colourful and tasty so that they don't get overlooked. A yogurt and fruit purée mousse provides softer texture after the more chewy savoury course.

Sliced and stoned green olives

Fruit mousse
Raspberry purée blended and set with yogurt and gelatine.
Recipe: p. 59.

Boiled sweet potato

Cherry tomatoes

Rattle munch
A cereal–coated beefburger arranged with sliced and stoned olives, cherry tomatoes and sweet potato.
Recipe: p. 57.

Grape juice drink
Unsweetened grape juice diluted with water is a richly coloured and flavourful drink.

MEAT LOAF MOTOR CAR

A slice of meat loaf forms almost a meal in itself with its blend of meat, vegetables and cereal. Whenever you bake one for the family, you can cut a piece for your child and shape it quickly and simply or use cookie cutters for fancy shapes. Add a few vegetables for extra colour and flavour. You can even arrange them in the loaf to make patterns by packing the meat mixture into the tin with alternating layers of chopped vegetables such as carrot rings, peas or sliced mushrooms. If you don't have any meat loaf, simply make the shape from a slice of bread spread with chicken liver mashed with yogurt and decorated with strips of cucumber or French beans. For a treat, bake a sponge with a layer of sliced fruit arranged underneath to give it extra moisture. Cut it into small pieces before serving.

Meat loaf
A slice of meat loaf served with courgette rings and chicory leaves. Also good served with a tomato sauce. *Recipe: p.58.*

Steamed courgette wheels

Wholemeal sponge
Sponge baked with a layer of pineapple and cherries. Use any available fruit. *Recipe: p.61.*

Chicory leaves

SOUPS

Fresh pea soup
(Recipe: p.56)

Borscht
(Recipe: p.56)

Spinach soup
(Recipe: p.56)

Lentil soup
(Recipe: p.57)

Thick and hearty soups are one of the best meals you can give to your child. They are also very quick and easy to make. For a soup in five minutes, purée any vegetables in a blender and then thin the mixture with water, milk or yogurt. Serve hot or cold depending on the season. For a thick soup, make a base of cooked pulses or potatoes and add vegetables and liquid for flavour. Try to keep a supply of stock in the freezer and use with any vegetables you have on hand. Small children tend to like their soups rather thick for easier eating.

Butter bean soup
(Recipe: p.56)

Carrot soup
(Recipe: p.56)

Chicken stock soup
(Recipe: p.56)

Tomato soup
(Recipe: p.57)

LIVER LOG CABIN

As liver is such a rich source of iron, do try to prepare it for your child regularly. For tenderness and flavour, use calf, lamb or chicken liver: about 50 g (2 oz), thinly sliced, should be enough. Take care to avoid overcooking the liver or it will be leathery and unappetizing. Gently grill or flash-fry it so it is brown on the outside and slightly pink when cut. Serve with a sauce to add moisture. For speed, simply sieve a halved tomato over the liver. This will remove the skin and pips and help to cool the liver down. The tomato purée and kiwi fruit are both sources of vitamin C. Try to serve iron-rich foods, particularly grains and pulses, with foods rich in vitamin C as this helps the body to absorb iron more efficiently.

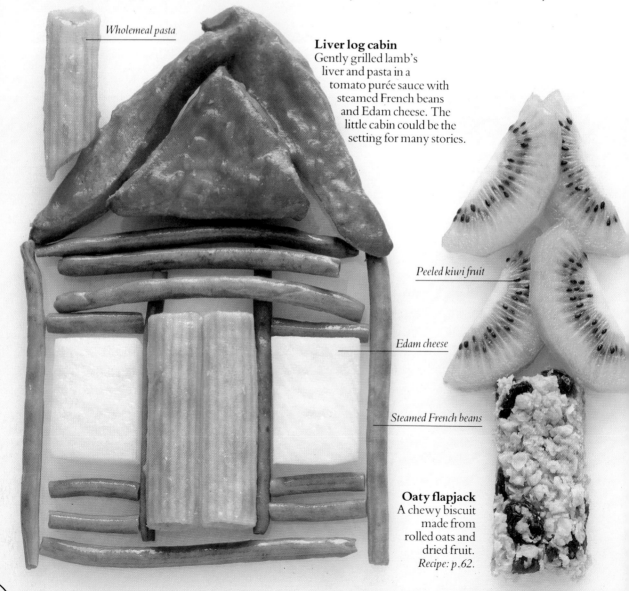

Wholemeal pasta

Liver log cabin
Gently grilled lamb's liver and pasta in a tomato purée sauce with steamed French beans and Edam cheese. The little cabin could be the setting for many stories.

Peeled kiwi fruit

Edam cheese

Steamed French beans

Oaty flapjack
A chewy biscuit made from rolled oats and dried fruit.
Recipe: p.62.

LITTLE SURPRISES

The surprises here are tender chicken livers hidden inside spinach leaf wrappings. Chicken livers have a mild flavour and delicate texture which will be preserved by gently sautéeing for about 4 minutes. Simply wrap the livers as they are or mix them with diced vegetables or cooked grain. The parcels are decorated with yogurt and tahini sauce, blended to taste. Tahini, made from crushed sesame seeds, is an excellent source of calcium and a good food for milk-haters. Further flavour, colour and shapes are provided by the stuffed celery and slices of banana oatmeal cake.

Banana cake cloud
A slice of banana oatmeal cake shaped with a pastry cutter.
Recipe: p.61.

Grated beetroot filling

Steamed celery stalk

Little surprises
Sautéed, chopped chicken livers wrapped in blanched spinach leaves and topped with a tasty blend of yogurt and tahini.

Blackcurrant drink
Diluted unsweetened blackcurrant juice. Avoid the bottled concentrated syrups, which are full of sugar in its various forms.

Spinach leaf stuffed with chopped chicken liver

Yogurt mixed with tahini

PICK-UP PASTA BOAT

Pasta is an excellent finger food: it is easy to pick up and available in a wide variety of attractive shapes and colours, as shown opposite. Serve it hot or cold with any kind of sauce. Here we've used a simple bolognese mixture of minced beef, chopped onions and tomatoes. Equally good sauces can be made from green or brown lentils, poultry, cheese and virtually any chopped or puréed vegetables. Slices of pineapple arranged as a sun and triangles of cheese as sails complete this nautical scene.

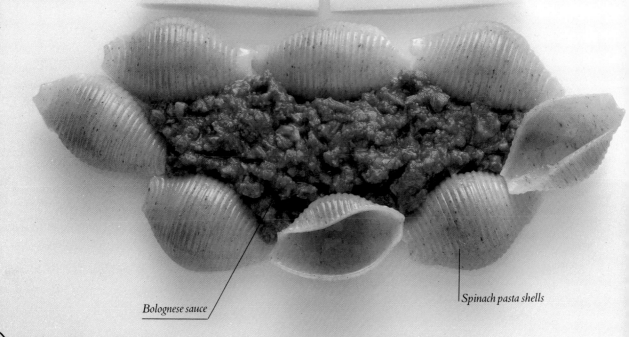

Green pepper flag

Pasta boat
A traditional meal of pasta and bolognese sauce is arranged as a picture-book sail-boat. The pasta and the cheese can be eaten as they are or used to scoop up the bolognese sauce.

Pineapple sun
Slices of fresh ripe pineapple make a shining sun.

Sliced Gouda sails

Bolognese sauce

Spinach pasta shells

TRAFFIC LIGHTS

This may look like a time-consuming meal to prepare but need not be if you have some vegetable purées in the freezer and a good assortment of pasta shapes. You can arrange purées and thick sauces in perfect circles by shaping them in a plain round pastry cutter. The jelly car is from a simple recipe and made car-shaped with a child's cookie cutter. This kind of meal will appeal to your child by making food interesting and enjoyable to eat.

Pasta sauces
Vegetable purées mixed with a little low-fat cheese or mashed potato to thicken make perfect accompaniments to pasta.

Tomato purée

Assorted pasta shapes

Cooked carrot purée

Lasagne strips

Spinach purée

Fruit jelly car
Made from unsweetened grape juice and fresh fruit.
Recipe: p.59.

Milk drink
Think of milk as a meal in itself and serve as a snack on its own or with light meals.

POLKA-DOT OCTOPUS

This is a fun and appealing way to serve beans but do take care when first introducing them to your child. Cook them thoroughly and serve in small quantities until your child's digestive system is accustomed to them. Once you are familiar with the many types, try to use beans often in salads, soups, casseroles, fillings and purées. They are colourful, rich in protein and pick up the flavours of other foods well. Serve the salad in a hollowed out roll and vary the ingredients according to what foods you have available. When possible, cook similar types of bean together to get different flavours, textures and colours in one dish.

Polka-dot octopus
A colourful salad of mixed beans with chopped avocado, tomato and sweet pepper in a light vinaigrette dressing served in a hollowed-out wholemeal roll.

Chopped tomato

Wholemeal roll

Chopped sweet pepper

Chopped avocado

Nutty banana
Banana coated in yogurt and finely ground nuts. Chill before serving.

Red kidney bean

Flageolet bean

Black-eyed bean

BEANY RING

Dried pulses are the edible seeds of vegetables and are rich in protein, iron, vitamins and minerals and low in fats. They need presoaking for 8–12 hours. Serve with whole grains for a complete protein meal.

Red kidney beans *must be fast boiled for at least 10 mins to destroy toxins.*
CT 45 mins/15 mins

Black-eyed beans *absorb flavours well.*
CT 45 mins/15 mins

Chick peas *must be cooked until soft.*
CT 60 mins/30 mins

Pinto beans *turn pink when cooked.*
CT 60 mins/30 mins

Flageolet beans *taste good and look pretty.*
CT 45 mins/15 mins

Cannellini beans *are good in tomato sauce.*
CT 45 mins/15 mins

Soya beans *must be boiled fast for the first hour.*
CT 2 hrs/50 mins

Aduki beans *are good mixed with rice.*
CT 45 mins/15 mins

Split peas *are good in soups and purées.*
CT 40 mins/10 mins

Haricot beans *are the original baked beans.*
CT 50 mins/20 mins

Lentils (whole and split) *need no soaking and are easily digested.*
CT 30 mins/15 mins

Butter (lima) beans *keep their shape well and are ideal finger foods.*
CT 60 mins/30 mins

CT = Boiling time/ pressure cooking time

Cooked beans mix well with all kinds of meat or vegetable stews and casseroles. For speed, you can use drained, canned beans or beans in a tomato sauce. Heat up with small pieces of assorted cooked vegetables and serve in a ring of mashed potato, pasta or cooked grain. For this dish, cooked brown rice was mixed with aduki beans and pressed into a ring mould. Shape with a cup or a shallow glass if you don't have a mould.

Cauliflower florets

Red kidney beans

Celery

Steamed celery

Tomato sauce

Brown rice and aduki beans

Beany ring
A wholesome flower with a centre of red kidney beans, celery and cauliflower florets cooked in a tomato sauce, ringed by aduki beans and brown rice and celery.

Strawberry milkshake
Milk blended with crushed strawberries is always a favourite summer drink.

BIRD'S NEST FEAST

This meal provides many different textures as well as a colourful arrangement. The peach, pineapple and sultana bird is sitting on a nest containing falafel – a tasty Middle-Eastern dish made from mashed chick peas. The salad nest consists of pitta bread, red cabbage and lettuce but any shredded vegetables, raw or cooked,

and bread strips would do. To make falafel, cooked chick peas are mashed, flavoured, mixed with breadcrumbs and rolled into balls. For extra crunchiness they can be coated in wheatgerm or cornmeal before cooking. They are delicious served with a dressing of yogurt and fresh chopped mint or yogurt and tahini.

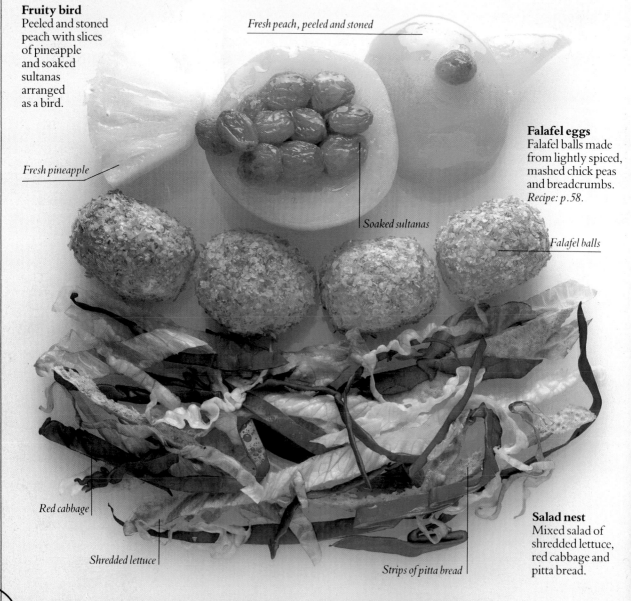

Fruity bird
Peeled and stoned peach with slices of pineapple and soaked sultanas arranged as a bird.

Fresh peach, peeled and stoned

Fresh pineapple

Falafel eggs
Falafel balls made from lightly spiced, mashed chick peas and breadcrumbs. *Recipe: p.58.*

Soaked sultanas

Falafel balls

Red cabbage

Shredded lettuce

Strips of pitta bread

Salad nest
Mixed salad of shredded lettuce, red cabbage and pitta bread.

DRINKS

Banana blended with milk

Milk with 1 tsp carob or cocoa powder

Apple juice and yogurt

Fruit, vegetable and milky drinks should be looked upon as liquid food and not merely refreshment. For pure refreshment, try to give plain water very early on otherwise children come to regard it as boring. Boil tap water until your child is at least six months old and dilute any juices with water by half. Check the labels on all commercial drinks to avoid those with added sugar and colourings.

Tomato juice

Mixed vegetable juice (p.59)

Orange juice

Yogurt blended with fresh mint

Mixed fruit juice (p.59)

Grape juice

Carrot juice

Apple juice

LEAFY PARCEL TRAIN

You can certainly involve older children in making these vegetable parcels. Younger ones will be intrigued with the idea of wrapping something up and unwrapping it again. Here, we have used cabbage leaves as the wrapping; an outer leaf, an inner leaf and a leaf of red cabbage. Spinach leaves would do just as well.

You can fill them with any vegetables, finely chopped, mixed with cooked grains and grated cheese. The little parcels are then cooked in vegetable stock or water in the oven. Fresh apple rings, celery and lightly steamed carrots provide crunchy texture and complete the picture of an old-fashioned steam engine.

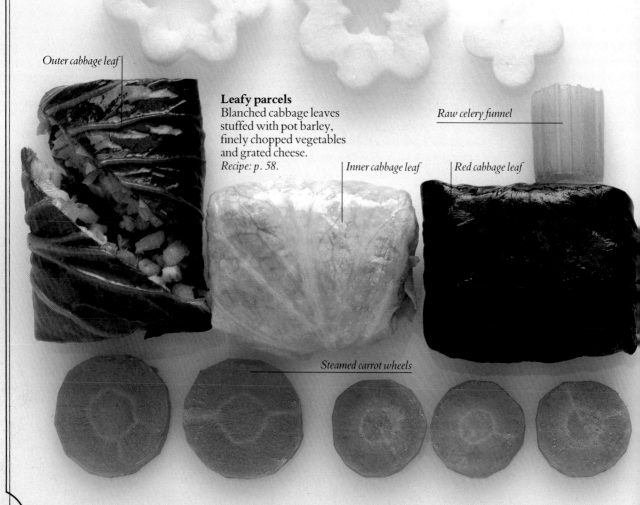

Apple clouds
Peeled and cored apple slices shaped into clouds of steam.

Outer cabbage leaf

Leafy parcels
Blanched cabbage leaves stuffed with pot barley, finely chopped vegetables and grated cheese.
Recipe: p. 58.

Raw celery funnel

Inner cabbage leaf

Red cabbage leaf

Steamed carrot wheels

VEGETABLE ROCKET

Courgettes, tomatoes and peppers are ideal for stuffing, and although we have used a vegetarian mixture here, you could add any leftover minced lean meat or cold chicken to the basic rice filling. If you are not preparing this dish for the rest of the family, you can speed up the cooking process by slicing the courgette in half lengthwise, steaming it and then mixing the pulp with the chosen filling, adding a little peanut butter, yogurt or tahini to bind the mixture. The meal is made more substantial with a small slice of wholemeal bread spread with low-fat cheese, a moon-shaped slice of pear and a mixed fruit tart.

Bread star
Wholemeal bread
spread with
low-fat cheese.

Pear moon
Peeled ripe pear, sliced and
shaped as a crescent moon.

Fresh pear

Vegetable rocket
Steamed courgette filled
with rice, diced red pepper,
sliced mushroom, courgette
pulp and peanut butter
thinned with milk.
Recipe: p. 58.

Mixed fruit tart
Wholemeal pastry case
filled with yogurt, fresh
pear and slices of dried fruit.
Recipe: p. 60.

Steamed courgette

Prune

Fig

Yogurt

Fresh pear

Dried apricot

STICKMAN FEAST

Few children will be able to resist this funny, welcoming figure or this combination of foods. The head is made from a mild version of the Mexican dip guacamole. Simply add a few drops of chilli sauce, fresh green chillis or chilli powder for serving to the rest of the family. Any selection of fresh, scrubbed vegetables sliced into strips can be used as dippers. Soften them by steaming when serving to children under 12 months old, particularly small pieces like these carrot eyes. Pancakes are always popular and can be made in batches for freezing. These have a filling of fruit purée but are equally good with savoury mixtures.

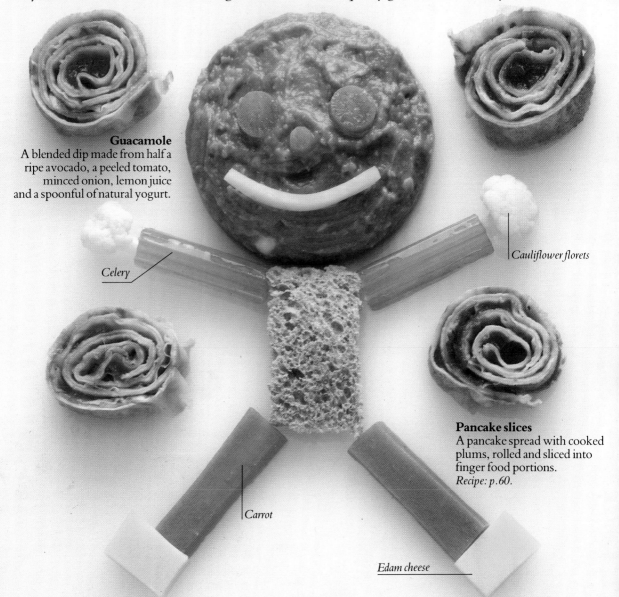

Guacamole
A blended dip made from half a ripe avocado, a peeled tomato, minced onion, lemon juice and a spoonful of natural yogurt.

Celery

Cauliflower florets

Pancake slices
A pancake spread with cooked plums, rolled and sliced into finger food portions.
Recipe: p.60.

Carrot

Edam cheese

DIP IDEAS

Smooth peanut butter mixed with soft tofu. Add a little lemon juice if the dip is too thick.

Low-fat cheeses make good sweet or savoury dips. This dip combines Quark and tomato purée.

Cooked chicken livers blended with cottage cheese make a mild and creamy dip.

Ripe avocado mashed with cottage cheese and lemon juice produces a delicately flavoured dip.

Interesting and colourful dips can be made from a wide variety of savoury and sweet ingredients. Serve them with raw or lightly steamed vegetables, homemade rusks or slices of fruit, but expect young ones to dip their fingers too! Use these dips as spreads for sandwiches or as fillings for tomatoes, celery stalks or small pastry cases. Your child will enjoy the experience of dipping and tasting and you will find that the rest of the family are just as keen to try these different ideas.

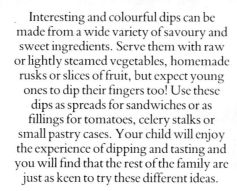

Hummus is made from chick peas and tahini. (Recipe: p.58).

Mashed, drained tuna fish mixed with curd cheese and lemon.

Chopped spinach blended with curd cheese and lemon juice makes a tasty dip and an interesting filling for pastry parcels.

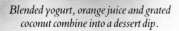

Blended yogurt, orange juice and grated coconut combine into a dessert dip.

Raspberry purée and Ricotta cheese blend together to make a naturally sweet dip. Good with sliced apple.

STIR-FRIED KITE

Stir-frying is the Chinese method of cooking foods quickly in very little oil. A wok is the traditional vessel for stir-frying but you can use a small frying pan over a low heat. Cook in a little polyunsaturated vegetable oil and use whatever fresh vegetables you have available:

any combination will make a tasty dish. We have added cubes of tofu (soya bean curd) which is an ideal food for young children being soft, mild in flavour, easy to digest and rich in protein and calcium. Wholemeal pitta bread and fresh banana balance the meal perfectly.

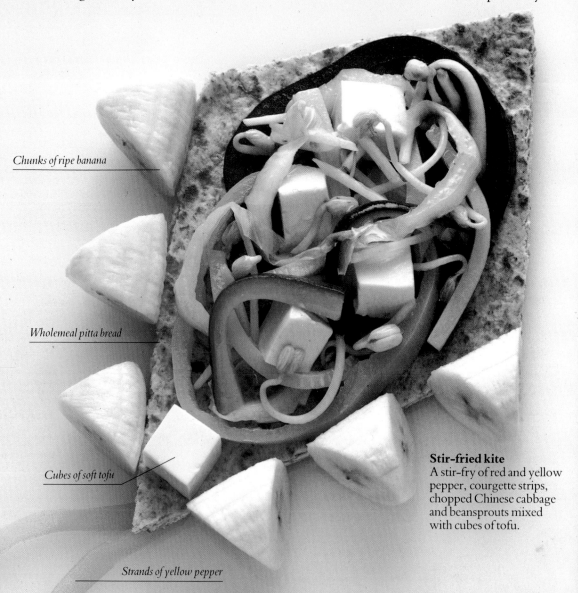

Chunks of ripe banana

Wholemeal pitta bread

Cubes of soft tofu

Strands of yellow pepper

Stir-fried kite
A stir-fry of red and yellow pepper, courgette strips, chopped Chinese cabbage and beansprouts mixed with cubes of tofu.

SANDWICH MAN

Don't overlook sandwiches as a quick, easy and nutritious meal for your child. Thin slices of wholemeal or other wholegrain bread can be cut with a decorative metal cutter for fun. Spread with any kind of homemade filling using soft or hard cheeses, grated vegetables and fruits, cooked meats, peanut butter, no-added sugar jams or bean purées – the choice is endless. Try not to use lashings of butter or margarine – a thin scraping is all that is needed. In fact, your child won't even notice if you use none at all on sandwiches. Excess use of butter or margarine is an undesirable habit that is learned all too often at a very early age.

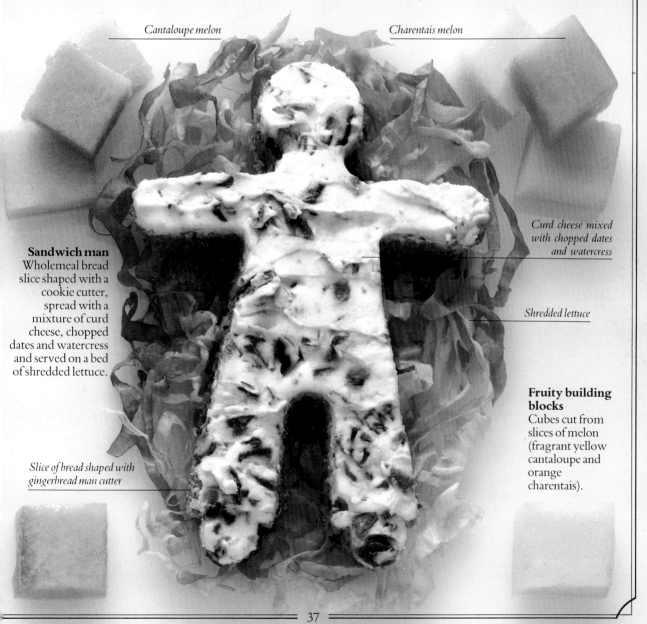

Cantaloupe melon

Charentais melon

Curd cheese mixed with chopped dates and watercress

Sandwich man
Wholemeal bread slice shaped with a cookie cutter, spread with a mixture of curd cheese, chopped dates and watercress and served on a bed of shredded lettuce.

Shredded lettuce

Fruity building blocks
Cubes cut from slices of melon (fragrant yellow cantaloupe and orange charentais).

Slice of bread shaped with gingerbread man cutter

PASTIE CRAB

Although we advocate wholemeal pastry most of the time, puff pastry can make a light and airy change. Pastry is always an excellent standby for savoury or dessert dishes and is a useful freezer food. Prepare it in small batches to freeze or buy additive-free commercial brands. Use to make tart cases, filled pies, pastie envelopes and any variety of shaped bases. We have filled this pastie with cooked spinach, cauliflower florets and sliced mushrooms but any combination of vegetables, cheeses, fish or meat will do. Test that the centre is well cooled before serving the pastie to your child and cut into strips to make it a finger food.

Wholemeal pastry

Pastie crab
Puff pastry filled with chopped spinach, mushrooms and cauliflower arranged as a crab with claws made from left-over pastry and slices of Edam cheese.

Edam cheese

Soft cheese shell
A spoonful of Ricotta cheese shaped like a shell using a tiny mould. Line the mould with cling film for easy removal.

Orange starfish
Orange segments arranged to look like a starfish. All pith and pips have been removed.

SAVOURY CONE

Left-over pieces of wholemeal pastry, shaped and baked quickly in the oven provide the base for this savoury cone. The topping is made from grated vegetables, including beetroot to give it a vibrant colour, bound together with a blend of yogurt, mayonnaise and ground almonds. Soft curd cheese or Quark would be speedy alternatives. The decoratively shaped pieces of fresh fruit and cheese are cut out with miniature cookie cutters. These finger foods allow children to choose which item to eat first at their own pace and help in the development of hand to mouth co-ordination. They can also be used as dippers in the soft topping.

Apple

Mango

Melon

Gouda cheese

Apple

Gouda cheese

Melon

Mango

Kiwi fruit

Savoury cone
Wholemeal pastry base with a scoop of grated apple and beetroot blended with yogurt, mayonnaise and ground almonds.
Recipe for pastry: p.59.

QUICHE FLOWER

Most adults were brought up to believe that the savoury part of a meal ought to be eaten first, but by serving savoury and sweet foods together you are offering your child a wider choice in flavours. There is no harm in starting a meal with something sweet, such as these slices of melon or any other pieces of fruit. But avoid letting your child fill up on sugary and fattening sweets, cakes, biscuits and desserts. Try to liven up otherwise plain looking dishes by adding brightly coloured garnishes. Here we've used watercress, which is rich in vitamin A and many minerals. Extra nutritional value is provided in a cup of carrot juice.

Quiche flower
Quiche with a wholemeal pastry base and a filling of egg custard, sliced leeks and tomatoes. *Recipe: p.60.*

Fruit petals
Slices of fresh mango arranged to look like a flower. Peaches canned in unsweetened juice could be used for the same effect.

Watercress

Carrot juice
Carrot juice is naturally sweet. Make from washed and scraped carrots. Serve diluted with a dash of lemon to preserve colour.

Mango stem

BAKING

*Banana oatmeal cake
(Recipe: p.61.)*

*Wholemeal sponge cake
layered with jam, curd
cheese and banana.
(Recipe: p.61.)*

*Plain oat biscuit
(Recipe: p.62.)*

*Wholemeal fruit scone served
with a moist filling of yogurt and
strawberry jam. (Recipe: p.60.)*

There is no good reason why children
should have any cakes and biscuits in their
first two years of life. However, outside
pressure from playgroups and parties will
doubtless encourage the inevitable taste
for sweet things so prepare for this by
getting your child used to less sugary
cakes and biscuits made from unrefined
ingredients. For example, substitute the
stronger tasting, dark brown, unrefined
sugars to cut down on the amount of
sugar required in recipes. Add sweeteners
like dried fruit and fruit juices when you
can and try to use wholemeal flour too.

*Oaty flapjack cut into small squares
for small hands. (Recipe: p.62.)*

*Date and nut cake keeps
well and tastes good.
(Recipe: p.61.)*

*Carrot cake made in tiny
paper cases for child-
sized portions.
(Recipe: p.61.)*

*Wholemeal sponge
marbled with carob
or cocoa.
(Recipe: p.61.)*

FOODS FOR TEETHERS

Children who are teething like to chew and suck to soothe their gums. Any piece of raw vegetable or fruit that is large enough to hold easily and can be sucked or chewed is a good teething food, particularly if it is chilled but not frozen solid. Wholemeal biscuits are attractive and give your child something hard to bite on at first and then become soft so they can be swallowed easily. If you have time, try to make your own teething biscuits and rusks. They are quick, inexpensive and free from unnecessary sugar. Most commercial varieties contain almost as much sugar as ordinary biscuits, and those advertised as "low-sugar" simply disguise their sugar content in the form of glucose – not a good start for first teeth! Older children may like to gnaw on a bone such as a spare-rib, a lamb chop or a chicken drumstick but take care not to offer anything with sharp edges, which can catch on inflamed gums. Although teething can be a wearing time for everyone, try not to resort immediately to using patent medicines and teething gels; nearly all contain a local anaesthetic that provides only a moment's relief and then has to be used again.

Baked spare-rib
Parboil first and check there are no sharp edges.

Chilled cucumber
Good for sucking on. Peel for young ones.

Teething biscuit
Tasty, chewable and covered in sesame seeds. *Recipe: p.61.*

Chilled raw carrot
Good for gnawing on. Give pieces that are too big to swallow.

Commercial rice cake
Contains no sugar, salt or other undesirable ingredients. Available from health food shops and some supermarkets.

Homemade rusks
Bake in a slow oven.
Add extra flavour with
grated cheese or yeast extract
before baking. Good for
staving off hunger. *Recipe: p.61.*

Stick of celery
Serve well chilled from the
refrigerator. Remove
fibrous strands first to
prevent choking.

Peeled and chilled raw apple
Nice to hold and rub on the gums.
Good to suck or bite on.

Plain oat biscuit
Hard for biting on but soon
becomes soft in the mouth
and easy to swallow.
Recipe: p.62.

Italian bread stick
Easy to hold and
good to bite on.

Orange juice

Yogurt

Grape juice

Layered ice-lolly
Made from grape juice,
yogurt and orange juice. Its
temperature will soothe
sore gums without freezing
them. *Recipe: p.59.*

Chilled pineapple core
Juicy and soothing for the gums.

43

FOOD ON THE MOVE

Most children become restless when strapped into a car seat or taken on a train for any length of time and it's a good idea to take a range of morsels for them to eat so you don't have to keep entertaining them. Don't pack messy foods or things that are difficult to hold. Cut sandwiches, small biscuits and pieces of fruit are best when you are on the move, even if it's just to cheer up your child when you are out shopping with the push-chair. Pastry cases are another good way of packaging food when you are travelling with children. Little packets of dried fruit, cubes of cheese and lightly steamed vegetable sticks are also good standbys.

Cored apple slices

Mini sandwiches
Take care not to overfill.
Cut into small squares for
easy handling.

Oaty flapjack
Cut to a manageable
size. *Recipe: p.62.*

Mini quiche
Pastry makes a good
container for all kinds
of food. *Recipe: p.60.*

Picnic Foods

The best picnics are full of surprises but are simple to unpack and serve. Cut a hole in a piece of pitta bread and fill it with salad, a homemade spread or thinly sliced meat. Cut the bread package in half when you reach your destination. Alternatively, cut a French loaf in half lengthwise, scoop out some of the crumbs and fill with a salad or spread. This can be sliced to make instant sandwiches when you arrive. Dips in tiny pots, plastic bags of prepared vegetables and slices of fresh fruit all provide the variety that makes for the most successful picnics. Don't forget to take plenty of drinks and water as well as a supply of wipes.

Carrot cake
A small slice of moist cake that won't collapse into crumbs. *Recipe: p.61.*

Flat bread sandwich
Pack in the filling so it doesn't fall out. Serve in small pieces that your child can hold.

Courgette

Pepper

Carrot

Celery

Tomato dip
A creamy dip made from curd cheese and puréed tomatoes. Take in a well-sealed jar with a supply of dippers.

Diluted orange drink
Drinks are essential for picnics and travelling. Mix on the spot.

EASTER FEAST

Easter shouldn't be solely about Easter eggs. You can make it a special occasion with other festive foods and shapes such as those shown here. Even older children will be excited by this Easter bunny, which should divert their attention from the ubiquitous chocolate eggs. The open sandwich has a topping of grated apple, carrot and cheese blended with yogurt and mayonnaise. Raisins and carrots provide the finishing touches. The curd cheese egg is easily made by rolling a teaspoon of low-fat soft cheese between the palms of your hands. You can decorate it with fresh chopped parsley or ground nuts.

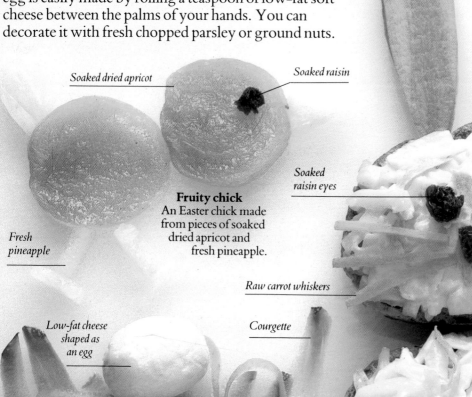

Trimmed raw carrot ears

Soaked dried apricot

Soaked raisin

French bread

Soaked raisin eyes

Fruity chick
An Easter chick made from pieces of soaked dried apricot and fresh pineapple.

Fresh pineapple

Raw carrot whiskers

Low-fat cheese shaped as an egg

Courgette

Cucumber

Carrot

Easter bunny
An appetizing spread of grated apple, carrot and cheese blended with yogurt and mayonnaise, served on slices of French bread.

EASTER TREATS

Start early by developing good habits where chocolate is concerned, particularly at Easter when there is so much of it around. Do make it a time for special treats but follow these ideas to cut down on the chocolate intake. Rather than offering pieces of solid chocolate, give fruit or biscuits that have been dipped in melted chocolate. Try using carob in place of chocolate; your child might like it and it contains less fat and refined sugar.

Curd cheese eggs flecked with carob or cocoa powder.

Dried apricot dipped in melted chocolate.

Seedless grapes dipped in melted chocolate.

Heart-shaped carob cookie (Recipe: p. 62.)

Peanut butter balls (Recipe: p. 63.)

Fruit tart decorated with grapes. (Recipe: p. 60.)

Carob-dipped strawberry

Cereal biscuits are always a special treat when dipped in melted chocolate. (Recipes: p. 62.)

Orange-flavoured, iced yogurt egg decorated with a bow of orange slices dipped in melted carob bar. (Recipe: p. 59.)

CHRISTMAS DINNER

There is no reason why your child shouldn't share in the family's traditional Christmas dinner, perhaps with one or two special treats like this frozen yogurt snowman, which you can prepare in advance. As Christmas dinner tends to be a feast of rich and hearty foods, give your child only a small portion. Children are usually excited by the atmosphere and the decorations and may not have much of an appetite. Arrange their food in morsels so they can feed themselves and you have more time to enjoy your meal.

Soaked dried apricot

Soaked sultana

Frozen yogurt snowman
Made from frozen yogurt, mild and refreshing.
Recipe: p.59.

Mini mincemeat tart

Roast potato

Sprouts

Christmas star
Arranged from steamed carrots, quartered sprouts, small roast potatoes and thin slices of turkey breast.

Turkey breast

Steamed carrot strips

CHRISTMAS TREATS

For Christmas you can prepare wholesome treats in advance and store them in airtight containers. A variety of tempting goodies can be made to replace traditional rich, high-fat and sugary Christmas fare. Invest in some seasonal cookie cutters so you can produce festive and appealing biscuits like these angels and bells. Try to use pieces of fresh fruit to add colour in tarts, and tone down rich mincemeat by adding chopped apple or grated carrots to your fruit mixture before baking in the oven.

Gingerbread Santa Claus (Recipe: p.62.)

Gingerbread angel (Recipe: p.62.)

Wholemeal almond biscuit (Recipe: p.62.)

Dessert oat biscuit (Recipe: p.62.)

Mincemeat tart with added chopped apple

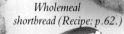

Wholemeal shortbread (Recipe: p.62.)

Mini palmiers (Recipe: p.63.)

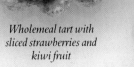

Wholemeal tart with sliced strawberries and kiwi fruit

Fresh date stuffed with Ricotta cheese

BIRTHDAY PARTY

As long as children enjoy a healthy diet most of the time there is no reason to exclude special treats on their birthdays and at other festive occasions. They may even come to associate such treats with special occasions only, and not demand or expect them every week. The most important thing about party food is its presentation. Most children are too excited to eat much and you will want to cut down on your preparation time. So select a limited menu carefully and incorporate good healthy food wherever you can.

Open sandwiches
Eye-catching, mouth-watering and quick to make.

Finger salad
Paper case filled with grated carrot, apple and beetroot decorated with a cherry tomato.

Tower sandwich
Made from brown and white bread layered with sliced tomato, watercress, curd cheese and chicken liver paté.

Open sandwich

Birthday cake
For a wholesome and appealing cake, follow one of our recipes and decorate with a topping of soft cheese, yogurt and grated orange. *Recipes: p.61.*

Open sandwich

Mini boat-shaped quiche
Cheese and egg custard filling and colourful garnish of cress. *Recipe: p.60.*

Date and nut muffin
Baked in a petit-four case.
Ideal for small hands.
Recipe: p.61.

Gingerbread men
Always popular and can
be stored in an airtight
tin. Decorate with dried
fruit. *Recipe: p.62.*

Fruit mousse
A sugar-free grape juice
and yogurt jelly with fruit
purée mixed in and a blob
of thick yogurt for
decoration. *Recipe: p.59.*

SWEETS AND TREATS

To forbid sweets completely is unrealistic. To allow them in unlimited amounts is also wrong. When babies are young you won't have any problems with sweets, but as children grow older they will meet other children who eat sweets indiscriminately. Try to prepare for this by encouraging your child to appreciate less sickly treats and to accept sweet rationing and routines. If your child has a sweet treat with meals, it is less destructive on teeth than having sweet snacks throughout the day. Get your child into the habit of cleaning teeth after every meal and make it fun rather than a chore.

Apricot and orange ball
(Recipe: p.63.)

Orange jelly jube
(Recipe: p.63.)

Grape juice jelly jube
(Recipe: p.63.)

Date crunchy
(Recipe: p.63.)

FACTS ON FRUIT AND VEGETABLES

Fresh fruit and vegetables are the best to use for your child; frozen are the second best. If you use canned varieties, be sure to check the labels so you can avoid those with additives and extra salt and sugar.

Wash all fruits thoroughly after checking that they are ripe, and peel whenever possible until your child is about 18 months old. Then your child should become accustomed to chewing any thin peel on fruit as it is a good source of fibre. But stone and remove any pips before serving until your child is about 2 years of age. All citrus fruits contain vitamin C and yellow and orange fruits are also a good source of vitamin A.

Fresh vegetables, like fruit, are a rich source of nutrients as well as colours, flavours and textures. Wash all leaf vegetables and, when possible, scrub root vegetables rather than peeling them as most nutrients lie just beneath the skin. So they retain their full character and freshness, cook vegetables for the minimum amount of time as soon as they are prepared. Baking, braising stir-frying, steaming and boiling are all good methods, but try to use any cooking juices or water in stocks, soups and sauces. Although many vegetables can be served raw, when you are preparing salads and finger foods for children under 12 months, you may prefer to blanch some of them first for a few minutes (e.g. cauliflower) to make them less hard.

KEY TO SYMBOLS

ℇ	*Always peel*
◎	*Remove stones and pips*
✔	*Good raw*
✿	*Good in salads*
☞	*Must be cooked*
☆	*Good colour*
?	*An acquired taste*

FRUIT

APPLES	ℇ ✔ ◎ ✿	*Good all-rounders and as an instant snack. Purée with yogurt. Bake stuffed with dried fruit.*
APRICOTS	ℇ ✔ ☆ ◎	*Source of vitamin A. Serve ripe, peeled and sliced. Good fresh or dried.*
BANANAS	ℇ ✔	*A good first fruit. Easy to mash and mix with other foods. Good with cereals.*
BLACKBERRIES	✔ ☆ ?	*Must be ripe. Cook to a purée for juice, which stains. Good with other fruit.*
CHERRIES	◎ ✔ ☆	*Must be ripe. Juice stains so supervise eating.*
CURRANTS	✔ ?	*Must be ripe. Cook and purée for babies. Use sparingly, can be sharp to taste.*
DATES	✔ ◎ ✿ ☆	*Good fresh or dried. Remove stones and stuff with cheese.*
DRIED FRUIT	✔ ☆	*Rich in minerals. Wash and soak to soften. Serve as snacks, desserts or as sweeteners.*
FIGS	ℇ ✔	*Fresh or dried. Good mixed with yogurt. Chop up for snacks.*
GRAPES	✔ ◎ ✿ ☆	*Choose seedless varieties. Peel if child cannot chew skin.*
GRAPEFRUIT	ℇ ◎ ✔ ✿	*Choose ripe ones. Remove all pith and never add sugar.*
KIWI FRUIT	ℇ ✔ ✿ ☆	*Rich in vitamin C and an attractive colour.*
LEMONS	ℇ ◎ ✔ ✿	*Use juice and grated peel in cooking and drinks. Juice prevents other raw fruit discolouring.*
MANGO	ℇ ◎ ✔ ☆	*Sweet and juicy. A source of vitamin A. Purée with milk for fruit dessert.*
MELON	ℇ ◎ ✔ ✿ ☆	*Many varieties. Ripe pieces are refreshing and have soft flesh.*
ORANGES	ℇ ◎ ✔ ✿ ☆	*Like all citrus fruits, a juicy source of vitamin C. Cut off all pith for babies.*
PAPAYA	ℇ ◎ ✔ ✿ ☆	*Also called pawpaw. Soft texture with lots of juice. Good for breakfast and in salads.*
PEACH/NECTARINE	ℇ ◎ ✔ ✿ ☆	*Serve poached or raw. Use halved as a container for fruit salads.*
PEARS	ℇ ◎ ✔ ✿	*Good raw or baked. Also good with cubes of cheese for snacks.*
PINEAPPLE	ℇ ✔ ✿	*Remove core and use for teething on. Juicy, fibrous fruit. Good in salads with beetroot.*
PLUMS	ℇ ◎ ✔ ☆	*Many varieties. Serve ripe ones raw or stew in a little water. Purée makes a good jam.*
PRUNES	◎ ☞ ☆	*Stew and serve with yogurt or purée to make a jam. Soak to remove stone.*
RASPBERRIES	✔ ✿ ☆	*Good cooked or raw when ripe. Use to flavour cakes and yogurt.*
RHUBARB	☞ ☆ ?	*Stew or bake with orange rind and juice or dried fruit instead of sugar.*
STRAWBERRIES	✔ ✿ ☆	*Must be ripe. Introduce around 12 months. Good in tarts or with fromage frais.*

VEGETABLES

ASPARAGUS	☞✿	*Good in soups, quiches, salads. Simmer for 10 minutes, serve the tips.*
AUBERGINE	ℰ ☞✿ ?	*Baked and puréed it has good creamy texture, especially mixed with mayonnaise.*
AVOCADO	ℰ ◎ ✓ ✿ ☆	*Good texture for babies. A rich source of unsaturated fat.*
BEANSPROUTS	✓ ✿	*Easily digested and full of nutrients. Good snack food. You can sprout your own at home.*
BEETROOT	ℰ ✿ ☆	*Good in soups, sandwiches, salads and drinks. May turn urine red so don't be alarmed.*
BROAD BEANS	☞✿	*Serve when young and white. Good in soups, casseroles and sauces.*
BROCCOLI	☞✿☆	*High vitamin C content. Good in soups and quiches. Avoid any with yellow tips.*
BRUSSELS SPROUTS	☞☆	*Simmer lightly or steam. Serve with cheese sauce. Choose young, small ones.*
CABBAGE	✓ ✿ ☆	*Stuff the leaves or use in soups and stews. Finely grate for salads.*
CARROTS	✓ ✿ ☆	*Rich in vitamin A. Sweet, colourful all-rounder. Use in drinks and for baking too.*
CAULIFLOWER	✓ ✿ ☆	*Easy to digest. Good in soups, sauces and salads. Use unblemished florets.*
CELERIAC	☞ ℰ ☆ ?	*Stores well. Lemon juice prevents discolouration. Good in soups and salads.*
CELERY	✓ ✿	*Remove stringy parts for babies. Stuff with soft cheese or purées. Use leaves too.*
CHINESE CABBAGE	✓ ✿ ☆	*Also known as Chinese leaves or Pak choi. Good stir-fried, mild flavour.*
COURGETTES	✿ ☆	*Steam and mix with tomato or leftovers for quick meal.*
CUCUMBER	ℰ ✓ ✿ ☆	*Peel and stuff with cheese. Grate in yogurt for a quick sauce.*
GARLIC	ℰ ✓ ?	*Use sparingly in cooked dishes.*
GREEN BEANS	☞✿☆	*Tender dwarf beans are best. Frozen are a useful standby.*
KOHLRABI	ℰ ✓ ?	*Cut off stems and cook like other root vegetables. Use raw grated in salads.*
LEEKS	ℰ ☞	*Steam, braise or stir-fry. Good in soups or any vegetable dish.*
LETTUCE	✓ ✿ ☆	*Many colourful varieties. Shred or use leaf as a food container.*
MANGE TOUT	☞✿☆	*Also called snow peas. Eat whole or stuff. Serve with lemon juice.*
MUSHROOMS	ℰ ✓ ✿ ?	*Cook larger mushrooms. Stuff with rice or cheese. Use small ones in salads.*
OKRA	☞ ?	*Soft, sticky flesh. Steam or sauté. Serve without stalks.*
OLIVES	◎ ✓ ✿ ☆ ?	*Rather salty, but many children love them. Green are milder than black.*
ONION	ℰ ✿	*Mince and use sparingly. Try milder varieties such as red onions.*
PARSLEY	✓ ✿	*Rich in vitamins, iron and minerals. Good as a garnish and in sauces.*
PARSNIPS	☞ ℰ	*Sweet flavour. Mash with carrots or potatoes. Purée or slice with meats.*
PEAS	✿ ☞	*Choose small tender peas. Purée for a bright green dip. Frozen are a good standby.*
PEPPERS	✓ ✿ ☆ ? ◎	*Steam or grill in skins and peel. Red tend to be sweeter, green are rich in vitamin C.*
POTATOES	☞✿	*Cook in skin to retain nutrients. Purée with carrots, beetroot or peas for colour.*
PUMPKIN	☞ ℰ ☆ ? ◎	*Bake, steam or sauté. Purée with cheese. Also good in pies.*
SPINACH	✓ ✿ ☆	*Rich in minerals. Serve young leaves raw. Cooks quickly. Good mixed with soft cheese.*
SQUASH	☞ ℰ ◎	*Easily puréed. Good with cheese or herbs, sautéed, or stuffed and baked.*
SWEDE	☞ ℰ ☆	*Boil and mash with yogurt. Use in soups or any savoury dishes.*
SWEET CORN	☞☆	*Cook thoroughly. Hard for babies to digest.*
TOMATOES	✓ ✿ ☆	*Very versatile and rich in vitamin C. Good stuffed. Grate or sieve to extract juice quickly.*
TURNIP	☞ ℰ	*Takes on other flavours well when cooked. Season with herbs.*
WATERCRESS	✓ ✿ ☆ ?	*Good source of vitamins and minerals. Use in soups, salads, sandwiches.*
YAM	☞ ℰ ☆	*Also known as sweet potato. Boil or bake. Good in casseroles or mashed with yogurt.*

WHAT TO INTRODUCE WHEN

The chart below is designed to give you an idea of when to introduce different foods to your child. The timings are approximate as children develop at such different rates and have individual tastes, so always be flexible and use the chart as a guide only. Gradually increase the texture of the foods you serve. Infant gums can be quite tough and many babies enjoy chewing well before teeth have appeared.

Start offering finger foods once your child's hand to mouth co-ordination is good enough to pick up objects and get them to his mouth. Initially, you will have to help so you can be sure that at least

something has been eaten rather than dropped on the floor, the high-chair seat or in the bib. But the more you let children do, the faster they will learn.

Always introduce new foods gradually, one at a time, so you can identify any food that might cause a bad reaction (see *Allergy*, opposite). If your child rejects a new food, go back to serving old favourites and try offering the new food again after a few days. But don't insist that new foods are eaten up.

As long as you serve a selection of foods from the categories listed below, you will be providing a good range of essential nutrients. There is

no need to get bogged down counting calories and proteins. Just try to ensure that some foods from each of the groups are eaten over weekly periods. Children's appetites vary according to their size, how active they are and whether they are going through a growing period. If they start to refuse food, don't panic, it's probably just a passing phase.

KEY TO TEXTURE

▫	*Blended or puréed*
▫	*Coarser: mashed or minced*
▫	*Small, soft pieces; finger food*
▫	*Chopped pieces and finger foods*

AGE IN MONTHS	3 ~ 4	4 ~ 5 5 ~ 6	6 ~ 7
CEREALS	*Fortified baby cereal*	*Non-wheat cereals: rice, oats, millet, barley, rye, soya. Cook in twice the volume of liquid*	*Wheat cereals, muesli, wheat products Bread, crispbreads, rusks*
DRINKS	*Water, apple juice*	*Fruit and vegetable juices, well diluted*	*Whole cow's milk*
VEGETABLES		*Cooked carrots, peas, beans, marrow, swede, pumpkin, celery, cauliflower, spinach, parsnip*	*Tomatoes (peeled or sieved at first) Potatoes (in addition to, not in place of other vegetables)*
FRUIT		*Cooked fruit (apples, pears, etc.) Ripe banana*	*Soaked dried apricots and other dried fruit (but avoid raisins and sultanas at this stage)*
DAIRY PRODUCTS			*Whole cow's milk Cottage cheese, soft and hard cheeses Yogurt, plain or with puréed fruit added*
MEAT			*White meat: chicken, turkey Liver: chicken, calf or lamb*
PULSES			*Tofu, lentils, peas*
FISH			*White fish, skinned and boned*
EGGS			*Egg yolk only*
SEEDS & NUTS			*Ground nuts, peanut butter, tahini*
LIMIT THESE FOODS		*Blackcurrant syrup drinks*	

Allergy An allergy to a particular food can occur at any age and cause any reaction from a skin rash to vomiting. The likelihood of your child suffering an allergic reaction is greater if there is a history of allergies in the family. However, if you introduce new foods one at a time, with one-week intervals between, you will recognize any symptoms and be able to consult your doctor. Certain foods such as wheat and egg whites are more likely to cause problems and should be introduced later. There has been much publicity about sensitivity to food colourings and flavourings. In fact, very few children react in an abnormal way as a result of these additives, but avoid them if you can.

Foods to avoid For safety, you should avoid giving foods that are easy to choke on (i.e. small, hard and easy to swallow) until your child is 2-3 years old and able to chew well. Other foods which may not be directly harmful to your child but should be limited because they offer very little nutritional value are listed below and at the bottom of the chart. Highly sweetened foods (jams, commercial desserts, condensed milk, biscuits, cakes, all sweets) Processed meats (salami, bacon, ham, meat pies, sausages) Saturated fats (cream) Canned foods with added salt or sugar. (Check all labels.) Syrup drinks and squashes Salty foods (stock cubes)

Storage Homemade food is better than packaged commercial foods because you know exactly what it contains. If you have a freezer, you can prepare larger quantities of food and freeze individual servings. Use plastic cartons with lids or ice-cube trays, transferring the food cubes to plastic bags once they are frozen. Defrost in the refrigerator or in the microwave. Eat or freeze any leftovers within 12 hours and always remove food from cans as soon as they are opened. Cook fresh meat or fish within 24 hours and eat fruit and vegetables within two days. Don't give your child any foods with mould or bruising: even if you cut it off, the mould can penetrate to the healthy-looking part of the food.

7 ~ 8 8 ~ 9	9 ~ 10 10 ~ 11 11 ~ 12	over 12 months
Whole grains Pasta	Grissini – breadsticks Wheatgerm	Bread with whole grains
Milk shakes		
Raw vegetable pieces. Serve in large chunks at first to avoid bits breaking off and being swallowed whole	More strongly flavoured vegetables e.g. broccoli, cabbage, leeks, onion, pepper	Salad leaves Sweet corn
Raw, ripe fruit, peeled and seeded	Sultanas soaked until soft	Once child can chew well, leave peel on Berries, small seed fruits
Milk shakes Frozen yogurt		
Lean red meat (lamb or beef)	Meat balls, meat loaf, beefburger	Well-cooked pork, no fat Processed meats
Beans, cooked until soft		
	Tinned fish, well drained Oily fish e.g. mackerel, tuna	Shellfish Smoked fish
	Whole egg and whole egg products (e.g. custard)	
Polyunsaturated oils		Whole nuts only after 3 years
Biscuits, scones, cakes, pastry, pancakes, fried foods	Butter, cream, ice-cream	Processed meats (sausages, salami, etc), honey, sweets

RECIPES

In this book, we have tried to make the recipes simple, foolproof and flexible. Don't hesitate to use alternative ingredients and to speed up the preparation time by using a food processor or blender whenever you can. Although we haven't made stipulations in each recipe, we recommend that you try to use wholemeal flour, polyunsaturated vegetable oils and raw brown sugar. Sugar should be avoided in all its forms but because raw sugars and brown sugars that have had molasses added have a stronger flavour than the white refined varieties, you can use a smaller amount to add sweetness to biscuits and cakes. We haven't used honey. It is just another form of sugar, albeit with a trace of minerals, and as it may contain harmful bacteria, it is better not to give it to children under 12 months. If you are making a dish for all the family and want to use salt, add it after removing your child's portion. Experiment with the flavours of herbs and spices instead and remember that what may seem bland to you is not to your child.

SOUPS

BORSCHT

Makes about 900 ml / 1½ pints

4 medium, cooked beetroots	15 ml (1 tbsp) lemon juice
600 ml (1 pint) milk	30 ml (2 tbsp) yogurt

1 Purée the cooked beetroot and combine with the milk.
2 Bring the mixture gently to the boil.
3 Remove from the heat and stir in the lemon juice. Serve warm or cold and decorate with a swirl of yogurt.

BUTTER BEAN SOUP

Makes about 1 litre / 1¾ pints

15 ml (1 tbsp) oil	900 ml (1½ pints) stock or water
1 onion, chopped	15 ml (1 tbsp) tomato juice or purée
1 carrot, chopped	1 bay leaf
1 celery stalk, chopped	
100 g (4 oz) butter beans, presoaked	

1 Heat the oil and soften the onion for about 3 minutes.
2 Add the other vegetables and cook gently for a further 3–4 minutes.
3 Add the drained beans, stock, tomato juice or purée and the bay leaf. Cover and simmer for 1 hour (or 20 minutes in a pressure cooker).
4 Remove the bay leaf and liquidize until smooth.

CARROT SOUP

Makes about 1 litre / 1¾ pints

450 g (1 lb) carrots, chopped	600 ml (1 pint) stock or water
2 celery stalks, chopped	300 ml (½ pint) milk

1 Simmer the carrots and celery in the stock or water for about 15 minutes, until soft.
2 Liquidize and reheat with the milk before serving.

CHICKEN STOCK SOUP

Makes about 2 litres / 3½ pints

1 chicken carcase or bones (and giblets)	2 litres (3½ pints) water
1 onion	1 tsp mixed herbs
1 carrot	1 bay leaf
1 celery stalk	

1 Place all the ingredients in a pot, bring to the boil and then simmer for at least 1 hour.
2 Allow the mixture to cool and then strain. Use as a stock or serve as it is with small cubes of bread floating on top or, for variety and extra flavour, reheat the stock with peas or diced vegetables. To make more substantial, add some cooked rice, barley, noodles or soup pasta.

FRESH PEA SOUP

Makes about 1½ litres / 2½ pints

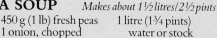

450 g (1 lb) fresh peas	1 litre (1¾ pints) water or stock
1 onion, chopped	150 ml (5 fl oz) yogurt
1 small lettuce, roughly chopped	

1 Simmer the peas, onion and lettuce in the liquid until cooked (20–30 minutes for shelled peas).
2 Liquidize until smooth.
3 Add the yogurt to a little of the soup, then combine this mixture with the rest of the soup. Reheat without boiling or the yogurt may curdle.

SPINACH SOUP

Makes about 900 ml / 1½ pints

450 g (1 lb) spinach, fresh or frozen	15 ml (1 tbsp) oil
1 small onion, chopped	900 ml (1½ pints) chicken or vegetable stock

1 Wash the spinach thoroughly, or thaw if frozen.
2 Sauté the onion in the oil to soften.
3 Add the spinach and the stock. Bring to the boil and simmer until tender.
4 Liquidize to make smooth.

TOMATO SOUP

Makes about 1 litre/1¾ pints

25 g (1 oz) margarine
1 onion, sliced
1 clove garlic,
   crushed

450 g (1 lb) tomatoes
600 ml (1 pint) stock
150 ml (5 fl oz) milk

1 Sauté the onions and garlic in the margarine until soft.
2 Add the tomatoes and stock. Cover and simmer for 15 minutes.
3 Take off the heat and stir in the milk.
4 Liquidize until smooth. Strain to remove tomato skins if necessary. Reheat without boiling.

LENTIL SOUP

Makes about 1½ litres/2½ pints

1 litre (1¾ pints)
   stock or water
50 g (2 oz) red lentils
   (or split peas or
   barley)
15 ml (1 tbsp) tamari

15 ml (1 tbsp) oil
1 onion, chopped
2 leeks, chopped
2 carrots, sliced
3 celery stalks,
   chopped
1 tsp cumin seeds

1 Sauté the onions, leeks, carrots and celery in oil to soften for about 5 minutes.
2 Add the rest of the ingredients. Cover and simmer for about an hour.
3 Liquidize until completely smooth.

SAVOURY DISHES

FISH FINGER TREE

Makes about 16

450 g (1 lb) white fish
   fillets
75 g (3 oz) cornmeal
   or wheatgerm
35 g (1½ oz) sesame
   seeds

1 tsp paprika
2 eggs, beaten
30 ml (2 tbsp)
   sunflower or
   sesame oil

1 Preheat the oven to 180°C (350°F) Gas 4.
2 Cut the fish fillets into 3 x 10 cm (1 x 4 in) fingers.
3 Mix the cereal, sesame seeds and paprika together.
4 Pour the oil into the beaten eggs and whisk together.
5 Roll each fish finger in the cereal mixture, then soak in the egg and oil. Roll again in the cereal until well coated.
6 Place on a greased baking sheet and bake in the oven for 10 minutes, turning after 5 minutes to cook evenly.

CHICKEN CHEWS

Makes about 16

450 g (1 lb) boned
   chicken (e.g.
   breast)
75 g (3 oz) cornmeal
   (or wheatgerm,
   oatmeal or rolled
   oats)

35 g (1½ oz) sesame
   seeds
1 tsp paprika
2 eggs, beaten
30 ml (2 tbsp)
   sunflower or
   sesame oil

1 Preheat oven to 180°C (350°F) Gas 4.
2 Cut the raw chicken into 3 cm (1½ in) cubes.
3 Coat and bake as described for **Fish fingers** (above).

TEDDY CROQUETTE

Makes about 8

25 g (1 oz) onion,
   chopped
25 g (1 oz) celery,
   chopped
3 tbsp parsley,
   chopped
100 g (4 oz) cooked
   potato mashed
   with 150 ml (5 fl
   oz) milk

350 g (12 oz) cooked
   turkey (or chicken)
25 g (1 oz) flour
75 g (3 oz) oatmeal
   (or rolled oats,
   wheatgerm or
   cornmeal)
1 egg, beaten with
   15 ml (1 tbsp) milk

1 Preheat oven to 180°C (350°F) Gas 4.
2 Mix together the first 5 ingredients and chill until ready to use.
3 Divide into 8 portions and roll or shape as desired.
4 Dip each portion into the flour and then the egg before coating in the cereal mixture.
5 Bake for about 10 minutes, turning over after 5 minutes to ensure even browning.

MERRY MEATBALLS

Makes 20-30

450 g (1 lb) lean
   minced beef
50 g (2 oz) rolled oats
1 small onion, finely
   chopped

1 egg, beaten
50 g (2 oz) grated
   cheese
1 tsp chopped parsley
   or oregano

1 Preheat oven to 180°C (350°F) Gas 4.
2 Mix all the ingredients together.
3 Shape the mixture into small balls about 2.5 cm (1 in) in diameter. To ease the shaping, dip your hands in cold water from time to time.
4 Place on a lightly greased baking tray and cook uncovered until light brown, about 20 minutes. Turn after 10 minutes to ensure even browning.
VARIATIONS
Substitute different cereals for binding, e.g. wheatgerm, bulgar wheat, barley or breadcrumbs. Combine with moist vegetables, e.g. grated carrots, courgettes or sliced mushrooms.

RATTLE MUNCH

Makes about 8

450 g (1 lb) lean
   minced beef
50 g (2 oz) bulgar
   wheat
1 small onion, finely
   chopped
1 egg, beaten

50 g (2 oz) grated
   cheese (or moist
   vegetables e.g.
   courgette)
1 tsp mixed herbs
100 g (4 oz) cooked
   brown rice (or
   other grain)

1 Preheat oven to 180°C (350°F) Gas 4.
2 Mix all the ingredients except the cooked rice.
3 Shape into flat rounds.
4 Roll each burger in the cooked rice (or other grain) before baking.
5 Cook, covered with foil, on a lightly greased baking tray for 20 minutes. Remove the foil for last 5 minutes.

MEAT LOAF CAR

225 g (8 oz) lean minced beef
1 onion, finely chopped
2 celery stalks, chopped
2 carrots, grated
1 clove garlic, crushed

1 egg, beaten
1 tsp cumin powder
2 tbsp fresh parsley, chopped
1 tbsp grated parmesan cheese
1 tbsp wholemeal breadcrumbs or wheatgerm

1 Preheat oven to 180°C (350°F) Gas 4.
2 Mix all the ingredients together thoroughly then pack into a small loaf tin.
3 Bake for about 1 hour.
VARIATIONS
To make the meat loaf more colourful, add a layer of thinly sliced vegetables before baking, or add a topping of grated cheese 10 minutes before the end of cooking.

FALAFEL BALLS
Makes about 20

275 g (10 oz) chick peas, presoaked
1 onion, finely chopped
1 clove garlic, crushed
1 egg, beaten

45 ml (3 tbsp) tahini
1 tsp cumin powder
100 g (4 oz) breadcrumbs (or wheatgerm, bulgar, or rolled oats)

1 Boil the chick peas in fresh water until soft (between 1 and 1½ hours or 30 minutes in a pressure cooker).
2 Preheat oven to 180°C (350°F) Gas 4.
3 Mash the chick peas with the onion and garlic to form a thick pulp.
4 Add the tahini, the beaten egg, the seasoning and the breadcrumbs (or cereal) and mix well together.
5 Divide the mixture into small balls and bake on a greased baking tray for 15-20 minutes.

LEAFY PARCELS
Makes 8

100 g (4 oz) pot barley
2 leeks, chopped
2 celery stalks, chopped
8 cabbage leaves
100 g (4 oz) mushrooms, chopped

50 g (2 oz) soft cheese (e.g. curd or cottage cheese) or grated cheese
1 tsp mixed herbs
1 egg (to bind if necessary)

1 Cover the barley in boiling water and cook for about 40 minutes until soft. Drain and reserve the liquid.
2 Preheat oven to 180°C (350°F) Gas 4.
3 Steam leeks and celery to soften.
4 Blanch the cabbage leaves for 2 minutes in a little boiling water, then drain.
5 Mix together the barley, chopped vegetables, herbs and cheese. Use an egg to bind the filling mixture if it is too crumbly.
6 Place about 1 tbsp of filling on each leaf, fold in the sides to the centre and roll up into a parcel.

7 Place in a lightly greased baking dish and add enough of the reserved barley stock to come half way up the parcels. Cover with foil and bake for about 30 minutes.

VEGETABLE ROCKET
Makes 8

4 courgettes
1 onion, finely chopped
1 clove garlic, crushed
1 red pepper, finely chopped
100 g (4 oz) cooked brown rice (or other grain)

15 ml (1 tbsp) smooth peanut butter (thinned with milk if necessary)
30 ml (2 tbsp) oil
300 ml (½ pint) stock or boiling water

1 Preheat oven to 180°C (350°F) Gas 4.
2 Blanch the courgettes for 3-4 minutes in boiling water.
3 Cut them in half lengthwise, scoop out the centres and chop up the flesh.
4 Sauté the onions, garlic, red pepper and courgette pulp for 5 minutes and then mix in to the cooked rice and peanut butter.
5 Fill the courgette shells with the mixture and arrange on a lightly oiled baking dish.
6 Cover and bake for 20 minutes.
VARIATIONS
Vary the filling according to what you have available and serve hot, or cold with a rice or other grain salad mixture and a yogurt topping.

HUMMUS

150 g (5 oz) chick peas, cooked (see **Falafel,** opposite)
1 clove garlic, crushed

1 tsp cumin powder
60 ml (4 tbsp) tahini
60 ml (4 tbsp) lemon juice
15 ml (1 tbsp) water

1 Blend the cooked chick peas, garlic, cumin, tahini and lemon juice.
2 If the mixture is too stiff, moisten with a little water to make the consistency of mayonnaise.

SMILEY FACE PIZZA

Base
225 g (8 oz) self-raising flour
50 g (2 oz) margarine
150 ml (5 fl oz) milk
50 g (2 oz) grated cheese

Topping
1 onion, chopped
1 clove garlic, crushed
15 ml (1 tbsp) oil
450 g (1 lb) tomatoes, skinned and chopped
30 ml (2 tbsp) tomato purée
1 tsp oregano or basil
75 g (3 oz) Mozzarella or grated cheese

1 Preheat oven to 200°C (400°F) Gas 6.
2 Sauté the onion and garlic in the oil to soften.
3 Add the tomatoes, purée and herbs (and any other ingredients you may want to use), cover and cook gently for 20 minutes.
4 Meanwhile rub the fat into the flour. Add half the grated cheese and gradually mix in the milk to make a scone dough.
5 Roll out the dough into a 25 cm (10 in) circle or 20×25 cm (8×10 in) rectangle. Place on a greased baking tray and sprinkle with remaining cheese.
6 Spread the topping over the base, decorate as desired and cover with Mozzarella.
7 Bake for about 30 minutes.

CHEESY MONSTER

Makes about 8 pieces

225 g (8 oz) red lentils
450 ml (¾ pint) water
1 onion, finely chopped
15 ml (1 tbsp) oil
100 g (4 oz) cheese, grated

1 tsp herbs
1 egg, beaten
25 g (1 oz) wholemeal breadcrumbs or wheatgerm

1 Preheat oven to 190°C (375°F) Gas 5.
2 Cook the lentils in the water until soft and all the liquid has been absorbed.
3 Sauté the onion in the oil until soft.
4 Mix all the ingredients together and press into a greased 23 cm (9 in) sandwich tin.
5 Bake for 30 minutes.
6 Cut out shapes for your child using pastry cutters. Serve hot or cold.

DRINKS AND DESSERTS

MIXED VEGETABLE JUICE

Makes about 350 ml/²⁄₃ pint

1 small beetroot, cooked and chopped
2 carrots, chopped

3 celery stalks, chopped
1 dessert apple, cored and chopped
200 ml (7 fl oz) water

Liquidize all the ingredients and strain through a sieve before serving.

MIXED FRUIT JUICE

Makes about ½ litre/¾ pint

4 large pieces of watermelon flesh, seeded
225 ml (8 fl oz) orange juice
squeeze of lemon

Liquidize all the ingredients and strain through a sieve before serving.

FRUIT JELLY

1 envelope unflavoured gelatine
50 ml (2 fl oz) cold water
100 ml (4 fl oz) boiling water

225 ml (8 fl oz) unsweetened fruit juice
225 g (8 oz) chopped peeled or puréed fruit (optional)

1 Pour cold water into a bowl and sprinkle in the gelatine. Leave to soak for 1 minute.
2 Add the boiling water to the bowl and stir to dissolve the gelatine.
3 Mix in the fruit juice and the fruit.
4 Pour into a mould or tray. Chill until firm. Cut out shapes as required.
VARIATIONS
Layered jelly Use different fruit juices and fruits in layers. Allow one layer to set before adding the next.
Fruit mousse Add 150 ml (5 fl oz) plain yogurt to the above recipe at stage 3.

LAYERED ICE-LOLLY

any unsweetened fruit juice
natural yogurt

1 Pour a layer of fruit juice into a mould, an ice cube tray or a small carton and place in the freezer.
2 When firm, insert a plastic spoon to act as the handle.
3 Once frozen, add a layer of yogurt or another juice.
4 Continue building up layers in this way.

FROZEN YOGURT

350 ml (12 fl oz) natural yogurt
175 ml (6 fl oz) orange juice
1 tsp grated orange peel

Mix all ingredients together well and freeze until solid. Set in shaped containers for novelty appeal.

PASTRY AND PANCAKES

WHOLEMEAL PASTRY

Makes 225 g/8 oz

175 g (6 oz) wholemeal flour
75 g (3 oz) margarine or butter
20 ml (1½ tbsp) water

1 Preheat oven to 200°C (400°F) Gas 6.
2 Rub the fat into the flour until it resembles fine breadcrumbs.

3 Add the water a little at a time until the mixture binds together without being sticky.
4 Roll out on a floured surface until about 3 mm (⅛ in) thick. Cut out into shapes with pastry cutters for mini tarts, or line a quiche or pie dish.
5 To bake blind, prick the base with a fork, cover with foil and sprinkle with dried beans. Bake for 15-20 minutes (30 minutes with a filling).

VARIATIONS

Fruit tarts Make pastry as above and line small tart dishes. Bake blind. Fill the cooked case with peeled, sliced and stoned fresh fruit, fruit purée or soaked dried fruit. Spread some yogurt or soft cheese on the base before adding the fruit, or use to decorate.

QUICHE FLOWER

pre-cooked pastry case in 18-20 cm (7-8 in) flan case	100 g (4 oz) chopped vegetables (e.g. mushrooms, leeks, tomatoes)
2 eggs	50 g (2 oz) grated cheese
300 ml (½ pint) milk	

1 Preheat oven to 180°C (350°F) Gas 4.
2 Combine the eggs, milk and chopped vegetables. Pour into the cooked flan case, sprinkle with cheese and bake for 20 minutes or until a knife inserted comes out clean.

DROP SCONES

Makes about 15

100 g (4 oz) flour	1 egg
1 tsp bicarbonate of soda	150 ml (5 fl oz) milk dried fruit
1½ tsp cream of tartar	

1 Sieve the dry ingredients into a mixing bowl.
2 Make a well in the centre and crack the egg into it. Gradually mix in the milk by stirring from the centre and drawing the dry ingredients into the egg and milk.
3 Heat a heavy pan and rub with a little oil to prevent the scones from sticking. Drop a spoonful of the mixture on to the hot surface.
4 Arrange fruit on the batter and turn over in one action when bubbles appear on the surface (after 1 or 2 minutes). Brown the other side.
5 Keep scones warm by wrapping in a clean cloth.
6 To freeze, allow them to cool thoroughly, layer each scone between sheets of greaseproof paper and put into a suitable container. Defrost at room temperature and toast lightly to heat through.

PANCAKES

Makes about 8

100 g (4 oz) flour
1 egg
300 ml (½ pint) milk
30 ml (2 tbsp) oil

1 Prepare the mixture as for **Drop scones**.
2 Heat an omelette pan and add a few drops of oil.
3 Pour in enough batter to coat the base. Cook for a minute or two until golden. Keep shaking the pan so the pancake remains loose. Lift with a spatula and flip over to cook the other side.
4 If cooking for the family, stack the pancakes as you cook them, placing a sheet of greaseproof paper between each one. Keep warm in the oven.

CAKES AND BISCUITS

FRUIT/CHEESE SCONES

Makes about 10

225 g (8 oz) wholemeal self-raising flour	150 ml (5 fl oz) milk
50 g (2 oz) butter or margarine	50 g (2 oz) dried fruit or grated cheese

1 Preheat oven to 250°C (450°F) Gas 7.
2 Rub fat into flour until the texture of fine breadcrumbs.
3 Add the dried fruit or grated cheese then gradually stir in the milk.
4 Turn the dough on to a floured surface and knead lightly to remove any cracks.
5 Roll out to about 2 cm (¾ in) thick.
6 Cut shapes with a small pastry cutter and place on a greased baking tray. Press all the trimmings together and roll out to make more scones.
7 Bake for about 10 minutes until golden.

CORNBREAD

275 g (10 oz) self-raising flour	225 g (8 oz) cornmeal
100 g (4 oz) sugar	4 eggs, beaten
2 tbsp baking powder	600 ml (1 pint) milk
pinch salt	100 g (4 oz) soft butter or margarine

1 Preheat oven to 200°C (400°F) Gas 6.
2 Mix all the dry ingredients together.
3 Add the lightly beaten eggs, milk and butter and mix for 1 minute until smooth.
4 Grease a 30 x 23 cm (12 x 9 in) baking tin and pour in the mixture.
5 Bake for 35 minutes. Cut into squares and serve warm.

WHOLEMEAL SPONGE

100 g (4 oz) soft margarine
100 g (4 oz) sugar
2 eggs, beaten
100 g (4 oz) wholemeal self-raising flour

1 Preheat oven to 180°C (350°F) Gas 4.
2 Line two 18 cm (7 in) sandwich tins with greased paper.
3 Cream the fat and the sugar together until light and smooth.
4 Gradually mix in the eggs and the flour, keeping the mixture smooth.
5 Divide the mixture between the tins and bake for 15–20 minutes, until firm. Leave to cool on a wire tray.
VARIATIONS
Chocolate or carob sponge Add 1 tbsp cocoa or carob powder. Mix and bake in the same way.
Marbled sponge Mix the ingredients as described above. Separate half the mixture and add 1 tbsp cocoa or carob powder to it. Spoon alternate mixes into sandwich tins and marble by running a knife through the mixture several times. Bake as above.
FILLINGS/TOPPINGS
Mashed banana
Sugar-free jam, fruit purée or sliced fruit
Curd cheese mixed with orange peel and a dash of orange juice to make smooth.

CARROT CAKE

100 g (4 oz) sugar
150 ml (5 fl oz) oil
3 eggs
200 g (7 oz) flour
4–5 large carrots, grated
2 tsp bicarbonate of soda
1½ tsp cinnamon

1 Preheat oven to 150°C (300°F) Gas 2.
2 Beat the oil into the sugar.
3 Add the eggs and beat well.
4 Sift the dry ingredients and add to the wet mixture.
5 Fold in the grated carrots.
6 Pour into a 23 x 32 cm (9 x 13 in) greased tin. Bake for about 1 hour.

BANANA OATMEAL CAKE

75 g (3 oz) rolled oats
225 ml (8 fl oz) milk
275 g (10 oz) flour
50 g (2 oz) sugar
5 tsp baking powder
2 tsp bicarbonate of soda
1 tsp cinnamon
1 tsp nutmeg
50 ml (2 fl oz) sunflower oil
2 eggs
2 tsp vanilla
4–5 mashed bananas

1 Preheat oven to 180°C (350°F) Gas 4.
2 Combine the oats and the milk. Set aside.
3 Mix the dry ingredients.

4 Add the oil, eggs, vanilla and banana to the oats and milk. Once mixed, add the wet mixture to the dry ingredients and stir only until the flour is moistened.
5 Fill a greased loaf tin and bake for about 90 minutes. Alternatively, fill small paper cases and bake for about 35 minutes, or until golden brown. This cake is at its best 2–3 days after making.

DATE AND NUT CAKE

225 ml (8 fl oz) boiling water
350 g (12 oz) chopped dates
275 g (10 oz) flour
1 tsp baking powder
1 tsp bicarbonate of soda
50 g (2 oz) sugar
65 g (2½ oz) finely chopped nuts
75 ml (3 fl oz) oil
1 egg, beaten
1 tsp vanilla

1 Preheat oven to 180°C (350°F) Gas 4.
2 Pour boiling water over dates in a bowl. Stir and cool.
3 Mix the flour, the baking powder and the soda. Add the sugar and the nuts.
4 Stir the oil, beaten egg and vanilla into the cooled date mixture.
5 Add the wet mixture to the dry ingredients, stirring just until the dry ingredients are moistened.
6 Place in a greased loaf tin and bake for an hour or until a knife inserted into the centre comes out clean. For muffins in small paper cases, bake for about half the time, until the centre springs back when pressed.

HOMEMADE RUSKS

Bread slices (old will do)

1 Heat oven on its lowest setting.
2 Slice bread into fingers or squares.
3 Place on a baking tray and bake in the oven for about 1 hour until they are dry and hard. Cool thoroughly and store in an airtight container.

TEETHING BISCUITS

Makes about 40

150 g (5 oz) wholemeal flour
150 g (5 oz) plain flour
1 tbsp wheatgerm
45 ml (3 tbsp) oil
200 ml (6 fl oz) milk
1 tsp molasses
3 tbsp sesame seeds

1 Preheat oven to 180°C (350°F) Gas 4.
2 Mix the flours and the wheatgerm.
3 Stir in the oil, the milk and the molasses. Make a dough.
4 Divide the dough in half. Place one portion in the centre of a 30 x 40 cm (12 x 15 in) greased baking sheet. Roll to fill the tray.

5 Sprinkle with half the sesame seeds and press into the dough. Cut into small squares or other shapes with cutters but do not separate.

6 Repeat the process with the other half of the dough on a second tray. Bake for about 20 minutes.

PLAIN OAT BISCUITS
Makes about 20

50 g (2 oz) flour
175 g (6 oz) oatmeal
50 g (2 oz) rolled oats
1 egg yolk

pinch of bicarbonate of soda
100 g (4 oz) butter or margarine

1 Preheat oven to 180°C (350°F) Gas 4.
2 Mix together the dry ingredients.
3 Rub in the fat to resemble fine breadcrumbs.
4 Mix to a firm dough with the egg yolk.
5 Knead lightly. Roll out to a thickness of 6 mm (¼ in).
6 Cut into shapes and transfer to a greased baking tray.
7 Bake for about 15 minutes or until darker in colour.

DESSERT OAT BISCUITS
Makes 15-20

175 g (6 oz) flour
35 g (1½ oz) coarse oatmeal
1 tsp baking powder

75 g (3 oz) butter or margarine
50 g (2 oz) sugar
45 ml (3 tbsp) milk

1 Preheat oven to 180°C (350°F) Gas 4.
2 Mix the first 3 dry ingredients together.
3 Rub in the fat to make like fine breadcrumbs.
4 Stir in the sugar and add the milk. Mix until the dough is firm but manageable.
5 Roll out thinly and cut into shapes.
6 Place on a lightly greased tray and bake for 20 minutes, until light brown. Serve with jam or topped with fruit and yogurt.

OATY FLAPJACKS
Makes 15-20

½ quantity.

100g
40g
75g

225 g (8 oz) rolled oats or muesli
75 g (3 oz) sugar
150 g (5 oz) butter, melted

2 1 tsp baking powder
50 g 100 g (4 oz) dried fruit and orange peel

1 Preheat oven to 150°C (300°F) Gas 2.
2 Mix the rolled oats, sugar and baking powder.
3 Add the melted butter, dried fruit and peel, and mix together well.
4 Pat the mixture into an ungreased 20 x 30 cm (8 x 12 in) tray. Bake for about 20 minutes, until golden brown. Cut into squares before cooling.

WHOLEMEAL SHORTBREAD
Makes 10-15

150 g (5 oz) butter or margarine
175 g (6 oz) wholemeal flour

50 g (2 oz) ground rice
50 g (2 oz) sugar

1 Preheat oven to 160°C (325°F) Gas 3.
2 Beat the butter until thoroughly soft, then gradually work in the dry ingredients to make a stiff dough.
3 Roll out until about 6 mm (¼ in) thick.
4 Cut into shapes or slices and bake on a greased baking tray. Bake for about 30 minutes, until tinged brown.

WHOLEMEAL ALMOND BISCUITS
Makes 15-20

175 g (6 oz) butter or margarine
100 g (4 oz) sugar
1 egg, beaten

100 g (4 oz) wholemeal flour
50 g (2 oz) ground almonds

1 Preheat oven to 180°C (350°F) Gas 4.
2 Cream the butter and the sugar until light and fluffy.
3 Gradually mix in the egg.
4 Fold in the flour and ground almonds and mix well.
5 Spoon out the mixture in small dollops on to a well greased baking tray. Bake for 10-15 minutes.

CAROB BISCUITS
Makes 15-20

100 g (4 oz) butter or margarine
50 g (2 oz) sugar
½ tsp vanilla essence

100 g (4 oz) flour less 2 tbsp replaced with 2 tbsp carob powder

1 Preheat oven to 190°C (375°F) Gas 5.
2 Cream the butter and the sugar until light and fluffy. Mix in the essence.
3 Stir in the flour sifted with the carob.
4 Drop teaspoons of the mixture, well apart, on to a greased baking tray. Bake for 10-15 minutes, until hard.

GINGERBREAD MEN
Makes 15-20

350 g (12 oz) flour
1 tsp bicarbonate of soda
2 tsp ground ginger
100 g (4 oz) butter or margarine

100 g (4 oz) sugar
45 ml (3 tbsp) molasses or black treacle
1 egg, beaten

1 Preheat oven to 190°C (375°F) Gas 5.
2 Sift the flour, soda and ginger. Rub in the fat until the mixture resembles breadcrumbs. Add the sugar.
3 Warm the treacle until it is easy to pour. Make a well in the centre of the dry ingredients and add the treacle with the beaten egg until well blended.

4 Knead lightly and then roll out on a lightly floured surface until about 6 mm (1/4 in) thick.

5 Cut out shapes and place on a lightly greased tray, well spaced. Bake for about 10 minutes until golden brown.

PALMIERS

Makes 16

225 g (8 oz) frozen
puff pastry,
thawed
3 tbsp strawberry
jam

1 Preheat oven to 220°C (425°F) Gas 7.

2 Roll out pastry to a 6 mm (1/4 in) thick rectangle.

3 Spread thinly with 2 tbsp of the jam.

4 Fold the long edges in to meet at the centre.

5 Spread with the remainder of the jam.

6 Fold in half lengthwise to conceal the folds.

7 Firm the pastry down with your hand, and cut into 6 mm (1/4 in) slices with a sharp knife.

8 Place on a moistened baking tray, cut side down and well spaced to allow them to spread.

9 Bake near the top of the oven for 10 minutes. Turn over and bake a further 3–4 minutes.

SWEETS

CHEWY FRUIT

400 g (14 oz) dried
apricots, soaked or
fresh fruit, peeled
and cored **or**

800 g (28 oz) tinned
fruit in natural
juices

1 Preheat oven to its lowest setting.

2 Purée the fruit and then cook it over a low heat for 5 minutes.

3 Cover a baking tray with cling film paper and spread the fruit in the centre. Spread evenly across the tray.

4 Bake in the oven for about 8 hours to become dry and chewy.

5 Peel off the cling film and cut into shapes. Store in the refrigerator.

JELLY JUBES

Makes about 20

4 envelopes
unflavoured
gelatine

350 ml (12 fl oz)
unsweetened fruit
juice
2 tsp lemon juice

1 Warm up the fruit juice, but do not boil.

2 Dissolve gelatine in a bowl standing over a saucepan of boiling water. Stir continuously until dissolved.

3 Stir the gelatine into the fruit juice. Remove from heat and add lemon juice.

4 Pour into a 10–20 mm (1/2–1 in) deep tray or individual small moulds. Stand until firm. Cut into shapes with metal cutters. Store in the refrigerator.

PEANUT BUTTER BALLS

Makes about 15

100 g (4 oz) smooth
peanut butter
50 g (2 oz) soaked
raisins
175 g (6 oz)
wheatgerm

40 g (1½ oz) dried
milk powder
25 g (1 oz) ground
nuts

1 Mix all the ingredients and roll into balls or eggs.

2 Refrigerate to help them keep their shape.

DRIED FRUIT BALLS

Makes about 20

50 g (2 oz) margarine
175 g (6 oz) dried
fruit
2 eggs, beaten

75 g (3 oz) puffed rice
65 g (2½ oz) ground
nuts

1 Melt all margarine then stir in the fruit and eggs and heat until thickened.

2 Stir in the cereal and nuts.

3 Leave to cool then roll into balls. Chill until firm.

APRICOT AND ORANGE BALLS

Makes about 24

450 g (1 lb) dried
apricots, chopped
1 medium orange,
peeled and
chopped

65 g (2½ oz) grated
coconut
65 g (2½ oz) ground
nuts

1 Mix all the ingredients, if possible mince them in a food processor.

2 Shape them into balls.

3 Chill until firm.

DATE CRUNCHIES

Makes about 20

100 g (4 oz) butter or
margarine
75 g (3 oz) chopped,
stoned dates

75 g (3 oz) dark
brown sugar
100–150 g (4–5 oz)
sugar-free
breakfast cereal

1 Mix butter, dates and sugar in a pan and cook over a low heat until the dates have softened.

2 Draw off the heat and add the breakfast cereal to make a stiff consistency.

3 Cool, then shape into balls. Roll in coconut to decorate if wanted.

INDEX

Allergy 55
Avocado 28, 34, 35, 53

Banana 6, 28, 52
Beans, general 28, 29
    Beany ring 29
    Bean salad 28
    Bean soups *56*
Beefburger 21, *57*
Beetroot 39, 53, *56*
Biscuits 41, 42, 47, 49, *61-3*
Bread 6, 9, 37, 43
Breakfast 6, 8

Cakes 41, 50-1, *60, 61*
    Banana oatmeal cake 41, *61*
    Carrot cake 41, 45, *61*
    Chocolate/carob cake 50, *61*
    Date and nut cake 41, *61*
    Marbled sponge 41, *61*
    Wholemeal sponge 22, 41, *61*
Carrot 27, 40, 53, *61*
    Carrot soup 23, *56*
Celery 25, 45, 53
Cereals 7
Cheese 12, 13, 35, 37, 38, 46, 47, *59*
    Cheese bake 13, *59*
Chick peas 29, 30, 35, *58*
Chicken 18, *57*
    Chicken livers 25, 35
    Chicken soup 23, *56*
Chocolate 47
Choking 4, 15
Christmas treats 49
Cornbread 7, 9, *60*
Courgettes 33, 53, *58*

Dips 35, 45
Dried fruit 8, 10, 15, 51, 52, 54, *63*
Drinks 5, 12, 25, 27, 29, 31, 40, 45, *59*
Drop scones 6, *60*

Easter treats 46-7
Eating patterns 4-5
Eggs 10, 11, 55

Falafel 30, *58*
Fish 14, 15, *57*
Fresh pea soup 23, *56*
Fruit 6, 8, 14, 16, 35, 37, 44, 52

Gingerbread men 49, 51, *62*
Grains, *see* Cereals
Granary bread 9

Honey 56
Hummus 35, *58*

Iced-lolly 43, *59*
Introducing foods 54, 55

Jelly 27, 51, *59, 63*
Juices 25, 31, 52, 55

Labels on food 5, 55
Leafy parcels 32, *58*
Lentils 13, 29
    Lentil soup *57*
Liver 24, 25

Mangetout 10, 53
Meatballs 20, *57*
Meat loaf 22, *58*
Milk 27, 29

Oat biscuits 8, 20, 41, 49, *62*
Oranges 8, 38, 52

Pancakes 34, *60*
Parsley 11, 53
Party food 50-1
Pasta 24, 26, 27
Pasties 17, 38
Pastry 38, 39, 44, *59*
Pear 11, 52
Picnics 44, 45
Pizza 12, *58*
Potatoes 16, 53
Prawns 17
Pulses, *see* Beans

Quiche 40, 44, 50, *60*

Raspberries 13, 20, 35, 52
Rusks 42-3, *61*

Salt 5, 56
Sandwiches 35, 37, 44, 45, 51
Scones 8, 41, *60*
Shellfish 17
Snow peas, *see* Mangetout
Soups 23, *56, 57*
Spinach 25, 27, 35, 53
    Spinach soup 23, *56*
Stir-frying 36, 52
Storage 55
Sugar 5, 41, 55
Sweets 47, 51, *63*

Tahini 25, *58*
Teething foods 5, 42-3, *61*
Tofu 5, 35, 36
Tomatoes 16, 17, 23, 45, *57*
    Tomato soup 23, *57*
Travel foods 44, 45
Tuna fish 16, 35
Turkey 18, 49, *57*

Vegetables 27, 28, 29, 32, 33, 34, 35, 36, 52, 53, *56, 57, 58*

Water 12, 31, 45
Watercress 40, 53

Yogurt desserts 20, 21, 49, *59*

Pages in *italic* refer to Recipes

ACKNOWLEDGMENTS

Dorling Kindersley would like to thank the following people for all their help in producing this book:

Nutrition consultant
Karen Gunner

Photography page 1
Julie Fisher

Home economists
Janice Murfitt

Dolly Meers (pages 6, 22, 44, 45 and front cover)

Typesetting
SX Composing Ltd

Reproduction
Repro Color Llovet S. A., Barcelona